March
Patterns & Projects

Newbridge Educational Publishing, LLC
New York

The purchase of this book entitles the buyer to duplicate
these pages for use by students in the buyer's classroom.
All other permissions must be obtained from the publisher.

© 2000 Newbridge Educational Publishing, LLC,
11. East 38th Street, New York, NY 10016. All rights reserved.

ISBN: 1-58273-131-4

Photo Credit: (cover and title page) Norman O. Tomalin/Bruce Coleman, Inc.

Table of Contents

In Like a Lion and Out Like a Lamb Bulletin Board..5
The Letter "L"..9
Lion and Lamb Starch Art..10
Lion and Lamb Beanbag Toss..11

March Wind Bulletin Board..12
Wind Experiments..16
Words with Two Meanings..17
Blowing in the Wind..18

Lucky Leprechaun Movable Puppet..19
The Leprechaun Song..22
St. Patrick's Day Parade..23
Shamrock Hop..23
Match the Coins..25
Green All Around..25

Leprechaun Grocery-Bag Costume..26
Five Boastful Leprechauns Poem..30
St. Patrick's Day Scones..31
St. Patrick's Day Class Discussion..32

Jack and the Beanstalk Flannel Board Story..33
Jack and the Beanstalk Flannel Board..34
Planting a Beanstalk..38
A Story of Opposites..39
Bunches of Beans Art Project..40

Spring Planting Center..41
Planting Experiments..44
Spring Planting Terrarium..45
Growing a Garden Song and Game..47

Spring Garden Bulletin Board..48
Grow-a-Plant Book..52
Recommended Reading..53

Spring Science Centers..54
Life Science—Growing Up and Down..55
Earth Science—Making Rainbows..57
Physical Science—Attracting Others!..59

Birthday Party Parade Hats..61
Birthday Party Parade..62
An Unbirthday Party..66
Birthday Ice-Cream Cookie..67

Table of Contents (Continued)

Supermarket File-Folder Game **68**
What People Eat Class Book 73
Flower Fruit Salad 74
Food Group Bender Game 75

Hide-and-Seek Snail **76**
Snail Talk 80
Who's Hiding? 80

Art/Small Motor Skills/Sorting/Classifying

IN LIKE A LION AND OUT LIKE A LAMB BULLETIN BOARD

You need:
- crayons or markers
- scissors
- stapler
- gray and light blue bulletin board paper
- oaktag
- blue and yellow construction paper

1. Reproduce the lion, lamb, and cloud patterns on pages 6 through 8 five times each. Have children color and cut out.
2. Staple gray bulletin board paper onto the left half of the bulletin board and light blue paper onto the right half.
3. Make a raindrop pattern with oaktag. Have children trace and cut out using blue construction paper. Draw a big sun on yellow construction paper and have children cut out.
4. Staple the clouds, lions, and raindrops onto the gray half of the board and the lambs and sun onto the light blue side.
5. Encourage children to draw pictures and write or dictate stories about their favorite March weather and events.
6. Let children decide if their pictures and stories describe the stormy aspect of March or the calmer side of March. Staple the work onto the bulletin board accordingly.

Lion Pattern

Lamb Pattern

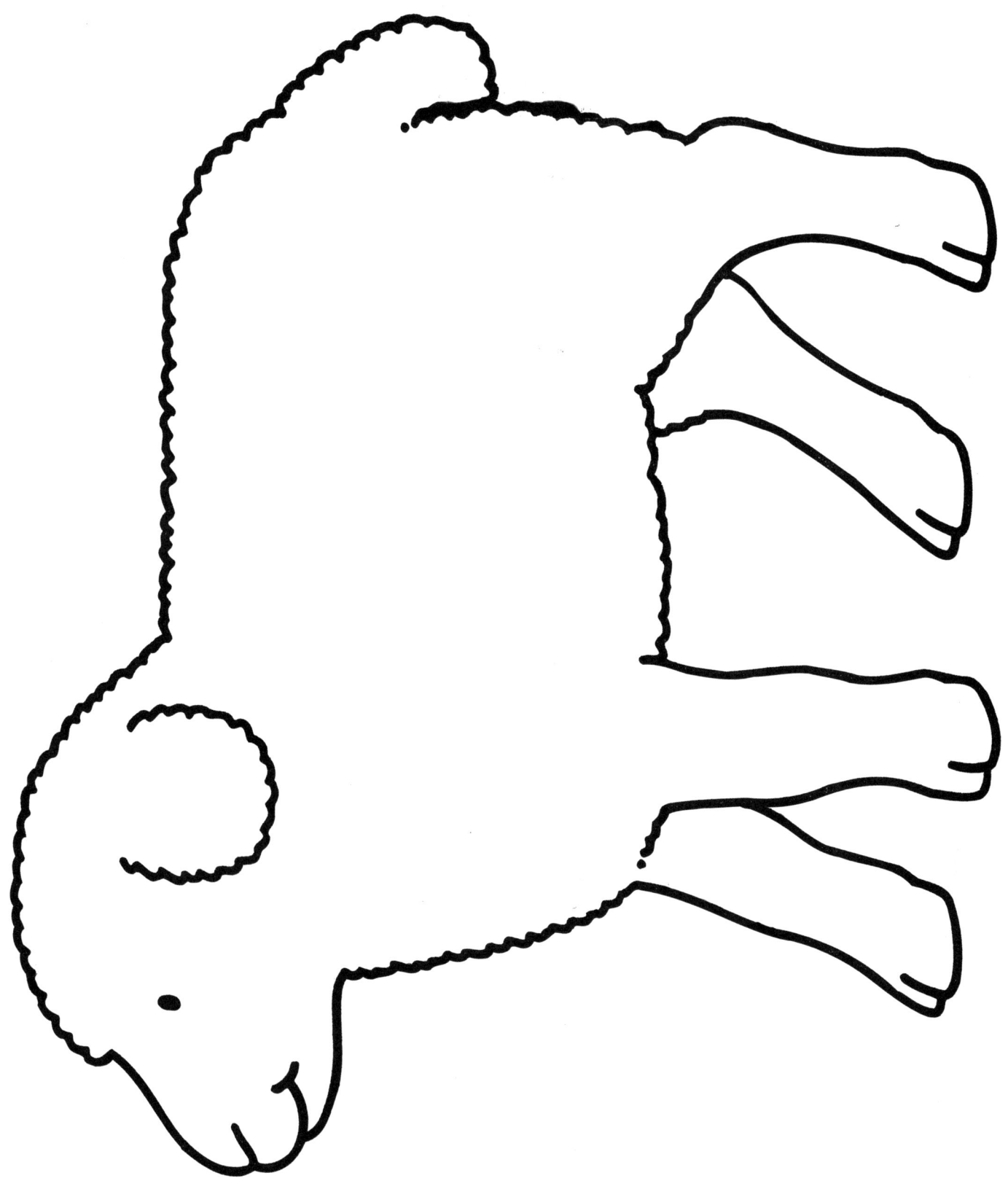

Newbridge

Cloud Pattern

Newbridge

Letter and Word Recognition/Vocabulary/Oral Communication

THE LETTER "L"

1. Help children learn about the letter "L" and the sound it makes by having activities that emphasize it on a special day. About one week before that day, gather children to tell them what will be happening.
2. Set the date with children and mark it on the class calendar. Ask them to bring in one thing from home on the special day that begins or ends with the "L" sound. Gather the class in a circle and instruct them to place their objects in the center of the circle. Allow each child to discuss his or her contribution.
3. Ask volunteers to look around the classroom and name objects that begin with the letter "L."
4. If desired, prepare a snack for the class that begins with the "L" sound (such as lemonade and lettuce).
5. Teach the class the following chant:

   Lion, lamb, lizard, lock,
   Letter, lamp, lollipop.
   Can you think of other stuff,
   Or have we already said enough?

6. Then ask each child to say a word beginning with the "L" sound. Continue the chant for as long as interest allows.

Art/Small Motor Skills

LION AND LAMB STARCH ART

You need:
- scissors
- waxed paper
- tape
- 10" strips of yarn
- liquid starch
- thread
- hangers

Optional:
construction paper

1. Reproduce either the lion pattern on page 6 or lamb pattern on page 7 for each child. Have children cut out.
2. Help each child lay a piece of waxed paper over his or her figure and tape the edges down, as shown.
3. Give children 10" strips of yarn to dip into a container of liquid starch. Then show children how to lay the yarn over the outlines of their figures. Continue this procedure until all the outside edges are covered. Make sure each child's yarn ends overlap so they will stick together when dry. Children may wish to trace over features as well.
4. When dry, have children gently remove the yarn figures from the waxed paper. Help children use thread to tie features to the outside edges of the pattern. For example, if a child traced over eyes for the lion, tie one end of a length of thread to each eye and tie the other end to the yarn at the top of the lion's head.
5. Help each child hang his or her figure from a hanger with thread. If desired, give children construction paper to make a banner to cover the hanger.

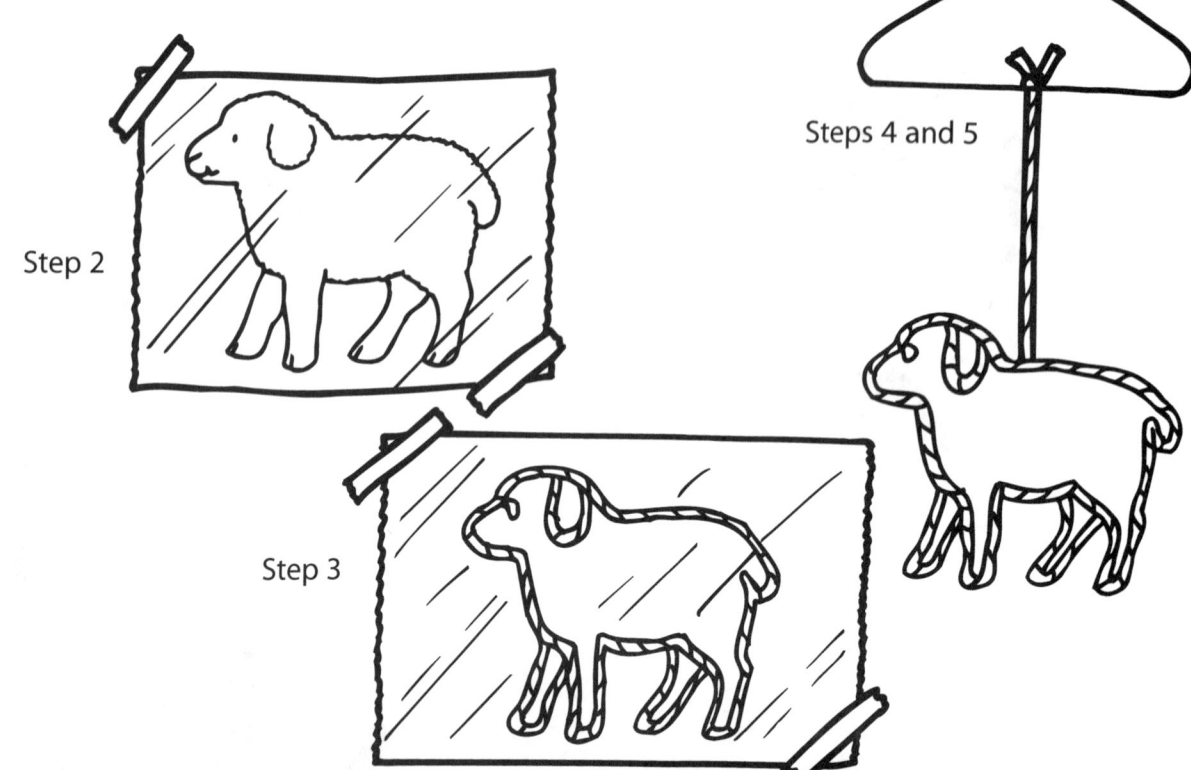

Addition/Large Motor Skills/Small Motor Skills/Art/Hand-Eye Coordination

LION AND LAMB BEANBAG TOSS

You need:
- crayons or markers
- scissors
- tape
- four socks
- beans
- rubber band

1. Reproduce the lion, lamb, and cloud patterns on pages 6 through 8 three times. Ask volunteers to color and cut out.
2. Tape the lions, lambs, and clouds randomly on the floor. On each lion have children write the number 1; on each lamb, the number 2; on each cloud, the number 3.
3. To make beanbags, cut off the top part of four discarded but whole socks. Fill the foot part with beans. Twist the tops and secure each with a rubber band, as shown.
4. Choose four players to write their names on the chalkboard. Then have each player try to throw the beanbag from a designated starting point onto one of the figures. Lions are worth one point, lambs are worth two points, and clouds are worth three points. If the beanbag lands on a figure, the player will read the number on it and write the number under his or her name. After five throws, players add their scores. The player with the most points wins and then challenges three other players.

Small Motor Skills/Reasoning/Classifying/Sorting

MARCH WIND BULLETIN BOARD

You need:
- bulletin board paper
- crayons or markers
- scissors
- stapler
- glue
- tape

1. Reproduce one pattern on pages 13 through 15 for each child. (Children can choose, but make sure each pattern is reproduced at least once.) Children color and cut out their patterns.
2. Help staple children's patterns to the bulletin board.
3. Invite children to name other items, besides those pictured in the patterns, that blow in the wind (e.g., flags, hats, paper, leaves, etc.).
4. Let children tape or staple to the bulletin board small samples or drawings of items that blow in the wind, such as small flags or leaves.

March Wind Pattern (Bunny)

Newbridge 13

March Wind Pattern (Boy)

Newbridge 14

March Wind Pattern (Squirrel)

Newbridge 15

Science/Observing/Drawing Conclusions

WIND EXPERIMENTS

Separate the class into small groups and help children perform the following experiments relating to wind.

Wind Distances

You need:
- small fan
- sheet of notebook paper

1. Set a small fan on a table or desk.
2. Fold a sheet of notebook paper. Stand it up 12" in front of the fan. Turn on the fan.
3. Ask children: "What happened to the paper?" (It blew away or was knocked over by the wind from the fan.)
4. Turn off the fan. Set up the paper again, 24" away. Turn on the fan. Did the paper move this time? If so, move the paper far enough away the next time so it will not blow over.
5. Ask children: "What did you learn about the wind from this experiment?" (Wind dies out after traveling a distance.)

Bubbles in the Wind

You need:
- container of soapy water
- bubble blowers
- small fan

1. Set up a small fan on a table or desk. Turn it on.
2. Have one group of children stand behind the fan and blow soap bubbles. (Make sure the children do not get too close to the fan.) Ask them to point to the general direction where their bubbles fall.
3. Have another group of children stand in front of the fan (also making sure they do not get too close.) Ask them to point to the general direction where their bubbles fall.
4. Ask the class: "Which bubbles traveled farther? Why do you think that happened?" (The wind from the fan blew them.)

Vocabulary/Word Meanings/Oral Communication

WORDS WITH TWO MEANINGS

Write these two sentences on the chalkboard, and read each aloud:
    March 21 is the first day of spring.
    The band will march on the field.

Let volunteers explain the two different meanings of the word *march*. Explain that sometimes a word can have more than one meaning. On the chalkboard write each pair of sentences below . After reading each pair aloud, have volunteers explain the different meanings of the underlined words.

A. March 21 is the first day of spring.
B. The frog is about to spring into the air.

A. Do you know how to tie your shoes?
B. The man is wearing a tie.

A. You can use a watch to tell time.
B. Please watch my bag for me.

A. This lamp gives off lots of light.
B. This box of feathers is light.

A. Should we go left or right?
B. Always eat the right foods.

A. You need a bat to play baseball.
B. A bat flew from the cave at night.

A. I need a pen to write with.
B. The sheep are all in their pen.

A. We took a trip to the park.
B. Don't run or you may trip.

A. I had an orange for lunch.
B. I have an orange crayon.

A. I saw a red rose in the garden.
B. The girl rose up and walked away.

Invite children to think of other words that have more than one meaning. Older students might make up their own sentences that illustrate the different meanings.

17

Name _____

BLOWING IN THE WIND

Circle the things that will blow in the wind.

Art/Small Motor Skills

LUCKY LEPRECHAUN MOVABLE PUPPET

You need:
- crayons or markers
- scissors
- glue
- oaktag
- hole puncher
- brass fasteners
- 12" and 18" pieces of yarn

1. Reproduce the leprechaun head and body patterns on page 20 and 21 once for each child. Have children color the parts and cut out.
2. Help children glue the parts separately onto oaktag and cut out.
3. Punch holes where indicated and use brass fasteners to attach the body parts, as shown. (Holes may need to be widened for better movement of the arms and legs.) Arms and legs should drop easily after lifting.
4. Have children glue the heads in place on the bodies.
5. Use a brass fastener to make a small hole at the top of each arm and leg where indicated.
6. Then help each child tie one end of a piece of 18" yarn to each arm. Tie one end of a piece of 12" yarn to each leg. All four yarns should meet below the puppet's waist. Knot the loose ends together, as shown.
7. To make the puppet move, have each child hold the leprechaun's head with one hand and pull down at the knot. The arms and legs will move up. When the knot is released, they will fall back down. By pulling only one piece of yarn, only the body part attached to that piece will move.
8. For activities, see The Leprechaun Song on page 22 and St. Patrick's Day Parade on page 23.

Step 3

Step 6

Leprechaun Movable Puppet Pattern

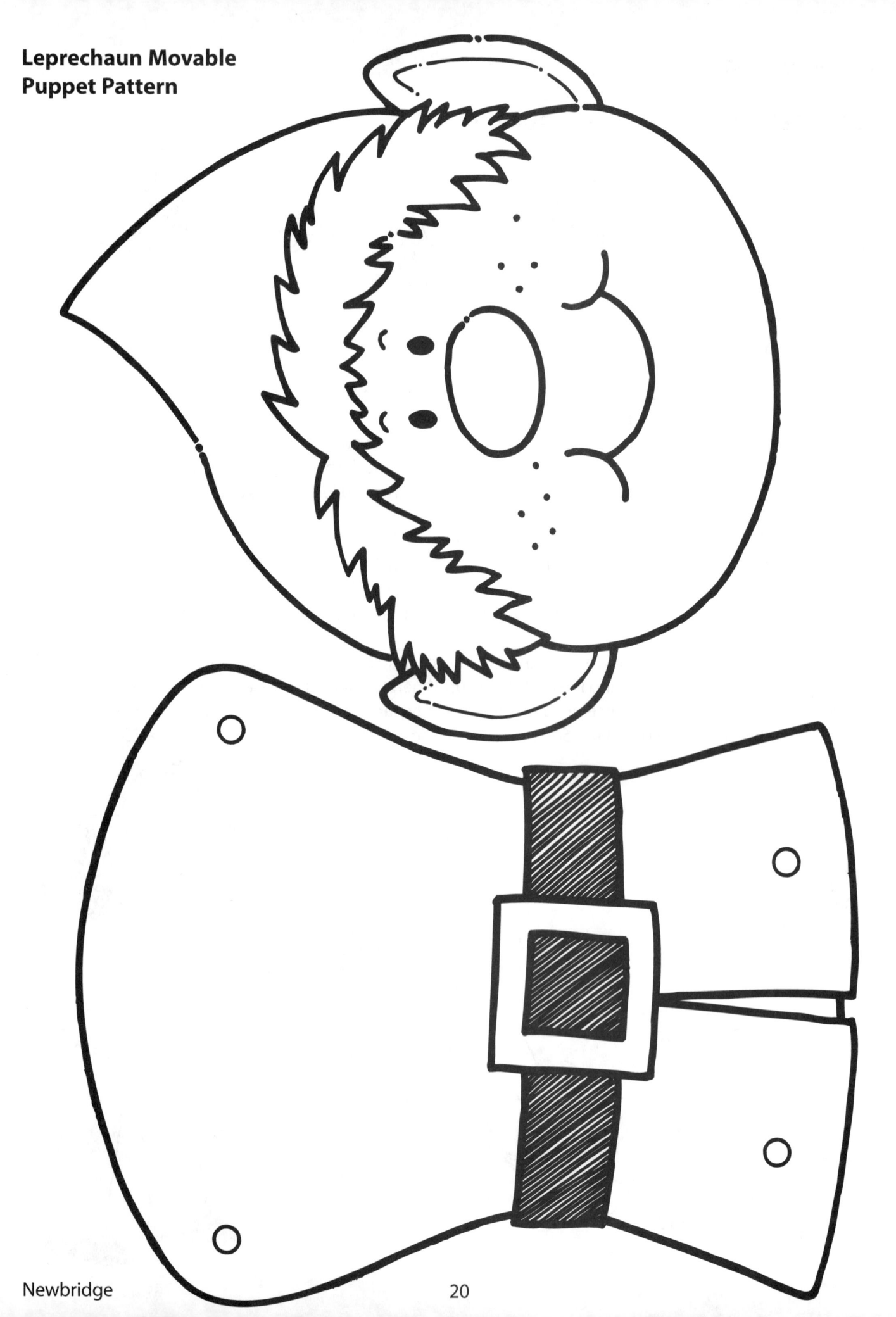

Newbridge

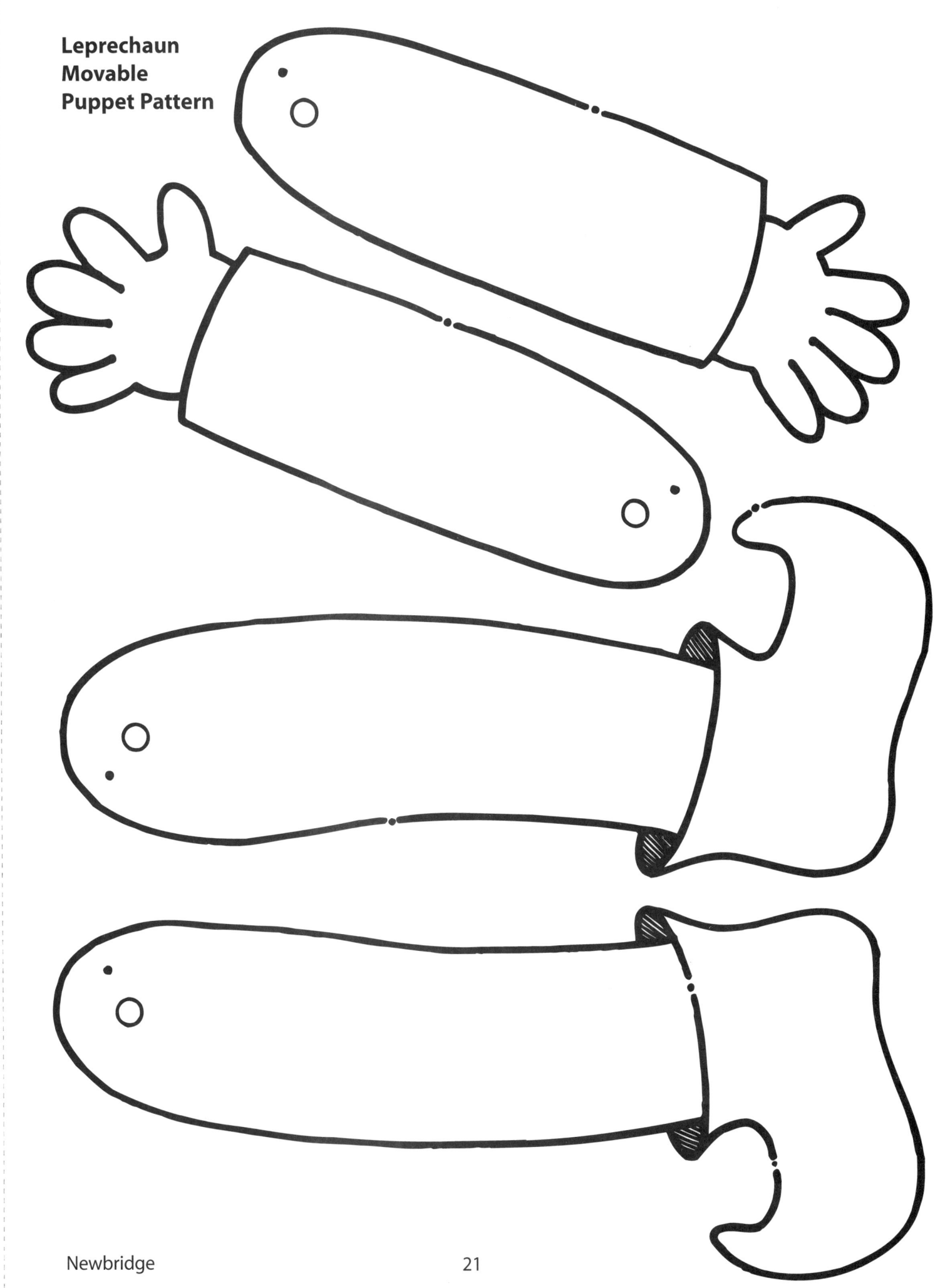

Large Motor Skills/Dramatic Play/Music

THE LEPRECHAUN SONG
(sung to the tune of "London Bridge")

Teach this song to the class and demonstrate how to move the leprechaun puppets to the words.

Leprechauns can dance a jig,
Dance a jig, dance a jig.
Leprechauns can dance a jig,
All day and night.
(move puppet up and down)

Leprechauns can wave their arms—
Oh, what a sight!
(move arm yarns)

Leprechauns can kick their legs—
With all their might.
(move leg yarns)

Leprechauns can jump so high—
High as a kite.
(make puppet jump)

Leprechauns can turn around—
Turn left and right.
(make puppet turn)

Leprechauns are tired now—
Turn off the light.
(lay puppet down on floor)

22

Large Motor Skills/Small Motor Skills/Art

ST. PATRICK'S DAY PARADE

1. Tell children they are going to hold a St. Patrick's Day Parade. Pick a leader (called the "Grand Marshal") and ask all children to wear green. Have each child use the shamrock pattern on page 24 to make a shamrock badge.
2. Children may parade through the school, outside, or into other classrooms with their puppets dancing. Have the class sing "The Leprechaun Song" and perform accompanying motions for other classes on the parade route.

SHAMROCK HOP

1. Reproduce the shamrock pattern on page 24 once for each child. Have children color and cut out. Laminate the shamrocks.
2. Place the shamrocks in a large circle and tape them on the floor, as shown.
3. Play some lively Irish music and tell children to dance, hop, or skip around the outside of the circle. When the music stops, each child must find a shamrock to stand on.
4. Remove one shamrock from the floor. Start the music again.
5. Have children dance, hop, or skip around the circle again. When the music stops, each child must find a shamrock to stand on. Since there is one fewer shamrock, one child will not be able to stand on a shamrock. That child is out of the game.
6. Remove another shamrock from the floor and continue the game until there is only one child remaining. That child is the winner.

Shamrock Pattern

Math/Matching/Money Sense/Color Recognition

MATCH THE COINS

You need:
- crayons or markers
- construction paper
- pushpins or tacks
- index cards

1. Make four "pots of gold" by drawing bowl shapes on construction paper, as shown.
2. Color the pots and tack them to a bulletin board, leaving the tops open.
3. On each of four index cards, write the name and value of a different coin (penny—1¢, nickel—5¢, dime—10¢, quarter—25¢). Use the cards to label each pot, as shown.
4. Make coins out of yellow construction paper, as shown. Make five each of pennies, nickels, dimes, and quarters. Label each coin appropriately.
5. Call children one at a time to place the correct coin in each pot of gold.
6. For older children, write a different amount of money on each pot. For example, you may write "36¢" on a pot. The child who places the money in that pot should use coins that total 36 cents.

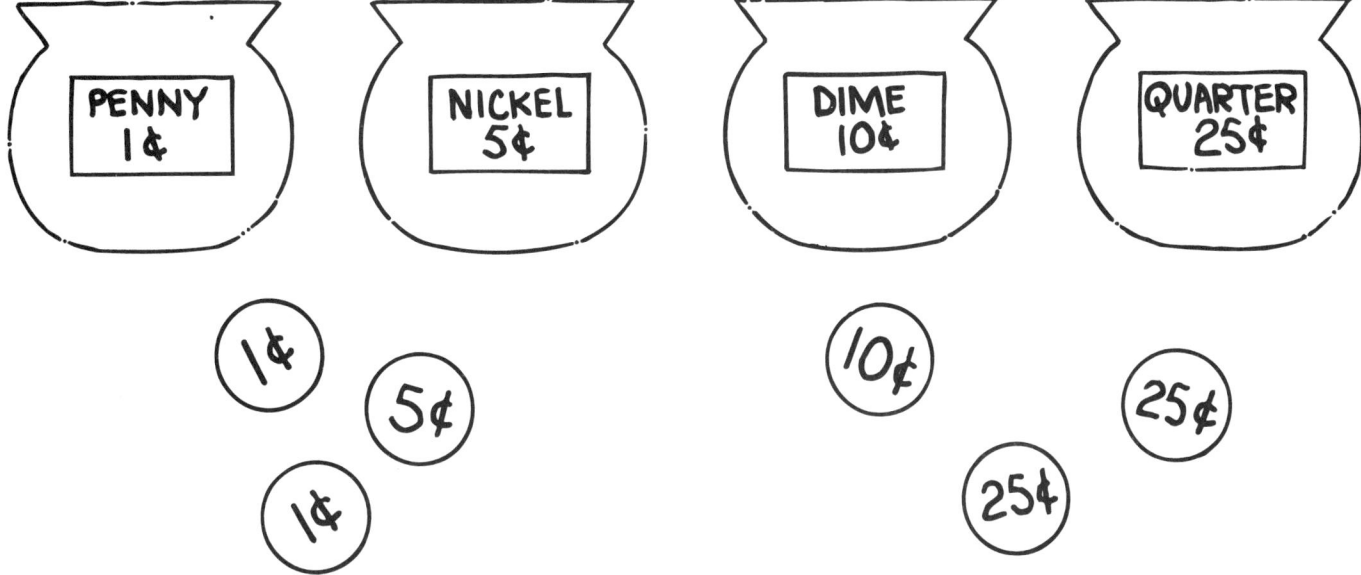

GREEN ALL AROUND

1. Have children form a circle. Choose one child to go first and name something in the room that is green. Continue around the circle until all the green things in the room have been named. Then ask children to think of green things outside the classroom.
2. Explain to the class that there are many different shades of green. Some of the different greenish colors are called aqua, turquoise, or lime green. Set up a "Green Table" in a corner of the classroom. Tell children that they may bring in any objects that are green or shades of green that they can find.

Art/Small Motor Skills

LEPRECHAUN GROCERY-BAG COSTUME

You need:
- crayons or markers
- scissors
- glue
- 2" x 24" strips of green construction paper
- stapler

1. Reproduce the hat, jacket, and legs patterns on pages 27 through 29 once for each child. Have children color and cut out.
2. Give each child a large brown paper bag. Help each child cut a hole in the bottom of the bag large enough for his or her head to fit through. Then slit the bag up each side along the center fold lines.
3. Holding the bag upside down, have each child glue the jacket to the upper half of the bag and the legs to the lower half, as shown.
4. Help each child fold a 2" x 24" strip of green construction paper in half lengthwise. Then staple the strip around each child's head to fit.
5. Have each child staple the hat to the headband, as shown.
6. For activities, see Five Boastful Leprechauns Poem on page 30 and St. Patrick's Day Scones on page 31.

26

Leprechaun Grocery-Bag Pattern

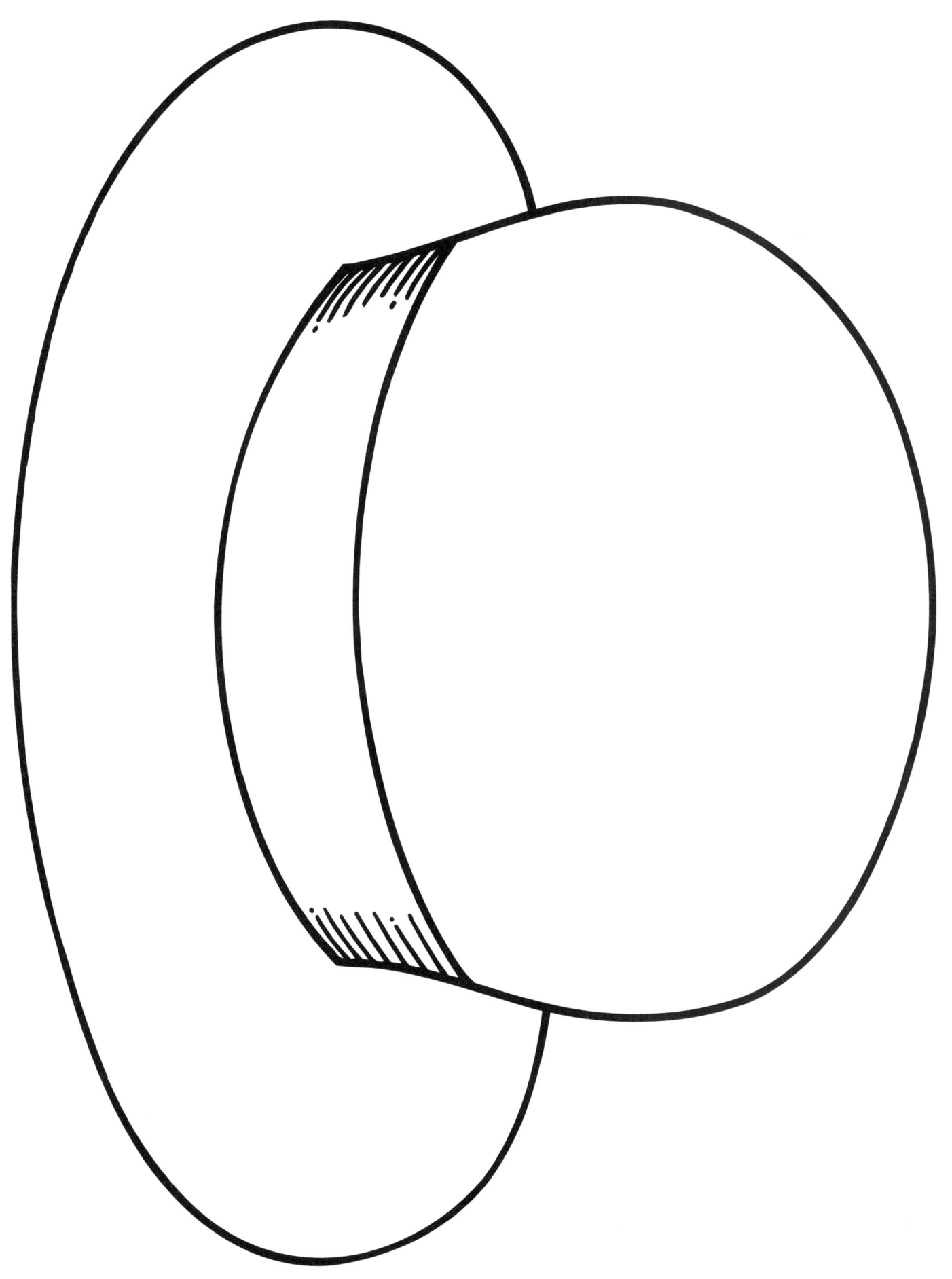

Leprechaun Grocery-Bag Pattern

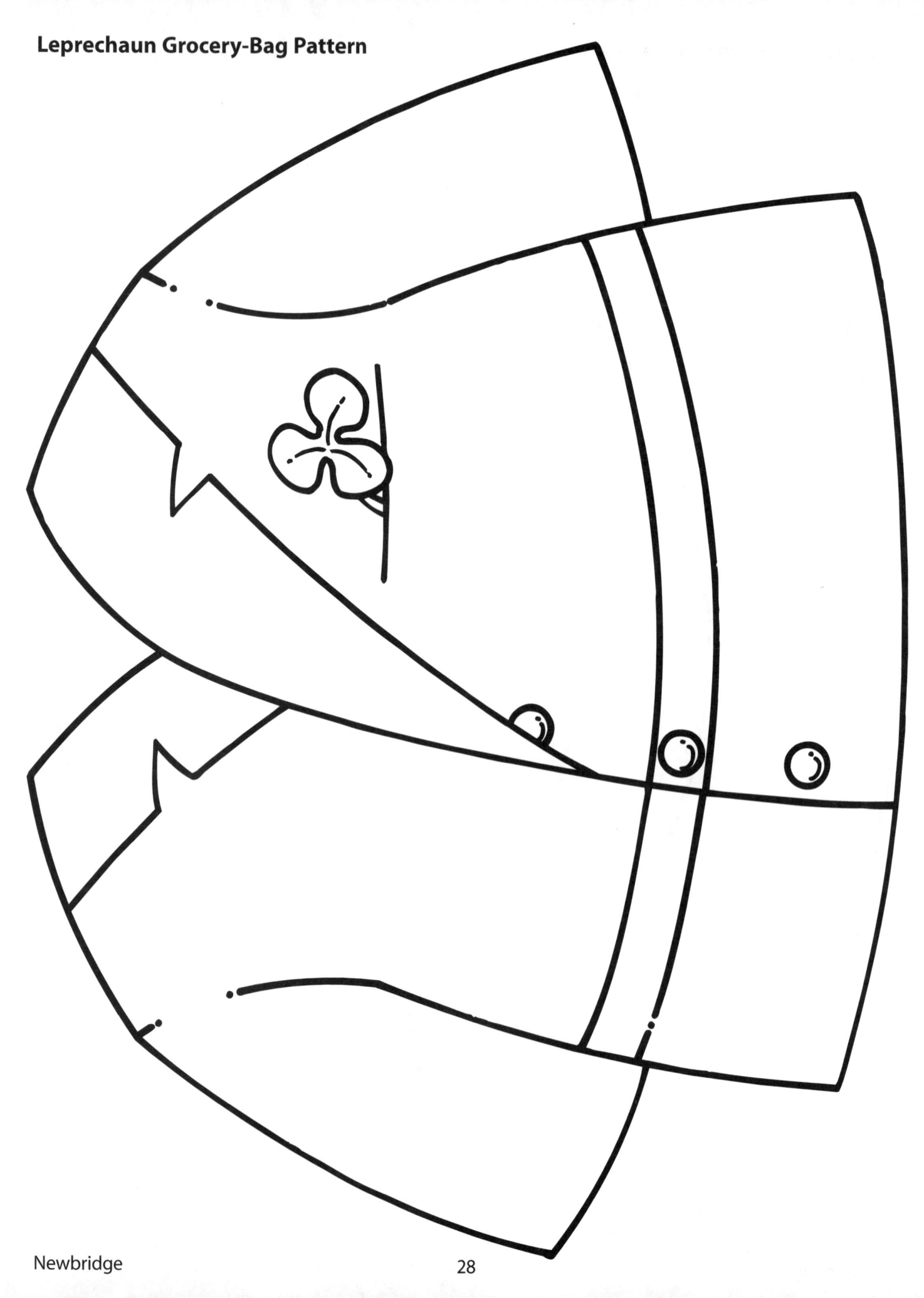

Newbridge
28

Leprechaun Grocery-Bag Pattern

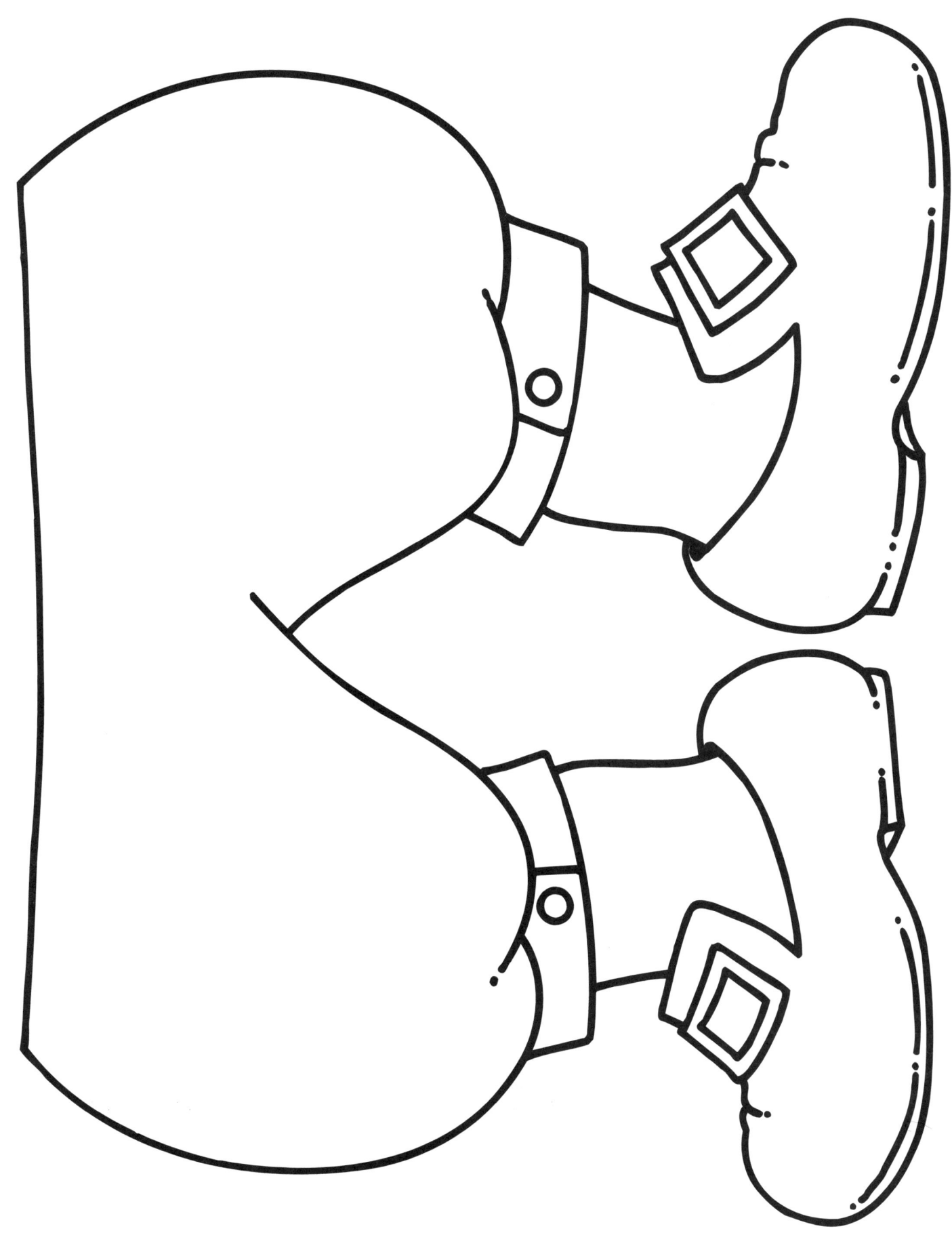

Newbridge 29

Oral Communication/Dramatic Play/Large Motor Skills

FIVE BOASTFUL LEPRECHAUNS POEM

Teach the class the following poem about five leprechauns who have just been caught by some humans. Ask volunteers to act out the poem wearing their leprechaun costumes.

Five boastful leprechauns making quite a fuss,
The first one said, "They'll never catch us!"
The second one said, "We're faster than they know!"
The third one said, "They're the slowest of the slow!"
The fourth one said, "They'll never wish on me!"
The fifth one said, "What's that up in the tree?"
Then down came the net, and feeling rather blue,
The five boastful leprechauns made every wish come true.

Cooking/Following Directions

ST. PATRICK'S DAY SCONES

Let children wear their leprechaun grocery-bag costumes (see page 26) when they make the following recipe. Serve as a snack at a St. Patrick's Day class celebration.

Yields: 1 dozen

You need:
- measuring cups
- large bowl
- sifter
- fork
- mixer or egg beater
- rolling board and rolling pin
- diamond-shaped cookie cutter
- cookie sheet
- brush
- 2 cups flour
- 4 teaspoons sugar
- 1/4 teaspoon salt
- 4 tablespoons butter
- 2 eggs
- egg white
- brown sugar
- cinnamon

1. Have children sift together the flour, sugar, and salt.
2. Show children how to cut in the butter using a fork.
3. Let children beat the eggs and add to the mixture. Cream well.
4. Help children pat or roll the dough on a floured board to 1/2" thickness.
5. Let children use a diamond-shaped cookie cutter to cut the dough. Place on a greased cookie sheet 2" apart.
6. Have children brush dough with the white of an egg and sprinkle with brown sugar and cinnamon.
7. Bake at 425° F for 15 minutes.

Social Studies/Cultural Awareness

ST. PATRICK'S DAY CLASS DISCUSSION

1. Ask if anyone in the class is of Irish descent. Explain that St. Patrick's Day is a holiday that Irish people, and others around the world, celebrate. St. Patrick was a priest who helped the Irish people. The color green, which is the national color of Ireland, is used for decorations on St. Patrick's Day, and one of the symbols of St. Patrick's Day is the shamrock, a small green plant with three leaves.
2. Ask if anyone knows what a leprechaun is. Tell the class that leprechauns are mischievous fairies from Irish folklore. They are supposed to look like little old men and make wishes come true for humans. It is said that leprechauns are very rich, and if someone catches them, they must tell where their riches are hidden.
3. Ask children if they celebrate St. Patrick's Day at home with their families and describe the activities planned for that day. If possible, have children bring in photographs of past St. Patrick's Day celebrations or objects that symbolize Ireland.

Listening Comprehension/Literature Connection

JACK AND THE BEANSTALK FLANNEL BOARD STORY

Once upon a time, a boy named Jack lived with his mother in an old hut. They were very poor, and Jack often went to bed with an empty stomach. One day Jack's mother asked him to take their old cow to the market and sell her so they could buy some food.

Soon after Jack left with the cow, he was stopped by a strange little man. When the man heard that Jack was going to sell the cow, he offered to trade the cow for a surprise he had in his pocket. Jack loved surprises, so he decided to make the trade. Jack closed his eyes and held out his hand. He felt some small objects drop into it. Slowly he opened his eyes and saw five beans.

"These are magic beans," whispered the little old man. "Be very careful with them." Jack stared at his hand once again. When he looked up, the man was gone! So there was nothing for Jack to do but return home and tell his mother he had traded the cow for five beans. His mother was very angry. She took the beans and threw them out the window.

The next morning Jack woke up and looked outside. He could hardly believe his eyes! In the very place where his mother had thrown the beans grew an enormous beanstalk that stretched out of sight into the clouds.

Jack decided to climb the beanstalk. When he reached the top he saw a huge castle. Jack walked up to the tremendous door of the castle and knocked timidly. A giant woman opened the door. Jack said, "I'm very hungry. May I have something to eat?"

"Hush!" said the woman. "If my husband finds out there's a boy around here, he'll eat you up! Be quiet and come with me." Jack followed the woman to a huge kitchen and ate the bread and cheese she gave him. Suddenly Jack heard thunderous footsteps. "Quick! Hide! My husband is coming!" whispered the woman. She hid Jack in a kitchen cupboard.

"Fee, fi, fo, fum!" bellowed a deep voice, "I smell the blood of a little one!" Jack peeked out of the cupboard and saw a gigantic man. "You're just hungry," said the giant's wife. "Eat your dinner." Jack watched in amazement as the giant devoured 200 sausages, 100 potatoes, 50 glasses of milk, 25 loaves of bread, and 10 wheels of cheese! Then he called out to his wife to bring him his hen. The hen made a noisy squawk and then laid a golden egg! The giant put the golden egg in his pocket and lay his head down to rest. Soon he was fast asleep at the table, shaking the room with his loud snores. Jack crept out from the cupboard, grabbed the hen, and rushed out of the castle. He climbed down the beanstalk as fast as he could.

Jack's mother was so pleased to see him! She told Jack that the hen had belonged to his father many years ago, but that a terrible giant had stolen it. With the return of the hen, all their money problems would be over!

The next day Jack decided to return to the giant's castle. He climbed the beanstalk and knocked on the castle door. Jack convinced the giant's wife to let him inside. Soon he heard the thunderous footsteps approaching and the loud voice roaring, "Fee, fi, fo, fum! I smell the blood of a little one!" Again the woman hid Jack in the cupboard and fed the giant an enormous supper. Afterward, the giant called for his magic harp. The harp played beautiful music all by itself! After listening for a while, the giant fell asleep.

Jack sneaked out of the cupboard and took the harp. But the harp cried out when he touched it! This woke the giant, who looked up just in time to see Jack escaping from the castle. He ran after Jack. Jack scampered down the beanstalk, but the giant was right behind him. When Jack reached the ground, he grabbed an axe and began to chop down the beanstalk. As the beanstalk swayed back and forth the giant lost his balance and fell. The giant crashed through the ground and was never heard from again. And Jack and his mother lived happily ever after.

Listening Comprehension/Dramatic Play/Art/Small Motor Skills

JACK AND THE BEANSTALK FLANNEL BOARD

You need:
- crayons or markers
- glue
- oaktag
- scissors
- sandpaper scraps
- cotton balls
- construction paper

1. Reproduce all the story patterns on pages 35 through 37 once. Have children color the figures, mount on oaktag, and cut out.
2. Glue small sandpaper scraps to the backs of the figures.
3. Cut several puffy cloud shapes from oaktag and glue shredded cotton balls on the shapes to represent clouds. Glue sandpaper scraps to the backs of the cloud shapes.
4. Cut several strips from various colors of construction paper and glue sandpaper scraps to each. The strips can represent Jack's cottage, the castle door, Jack's hiding place, and so on. Then cut out a group of egg shapes from yellow paper and glue sandpaper scraps to the backs to represent the golden eggs.
5. Leave the story and flannel figures out so children can dramatize the story during free time. Encourage children to make up stories of their own featuring the story characters.

Jack and the Beanstalk Flannel Board Patterns

Jack and the Beanstalk Flannel Board Patterns

Jack and the Beanstalk Flannel Board Patterns

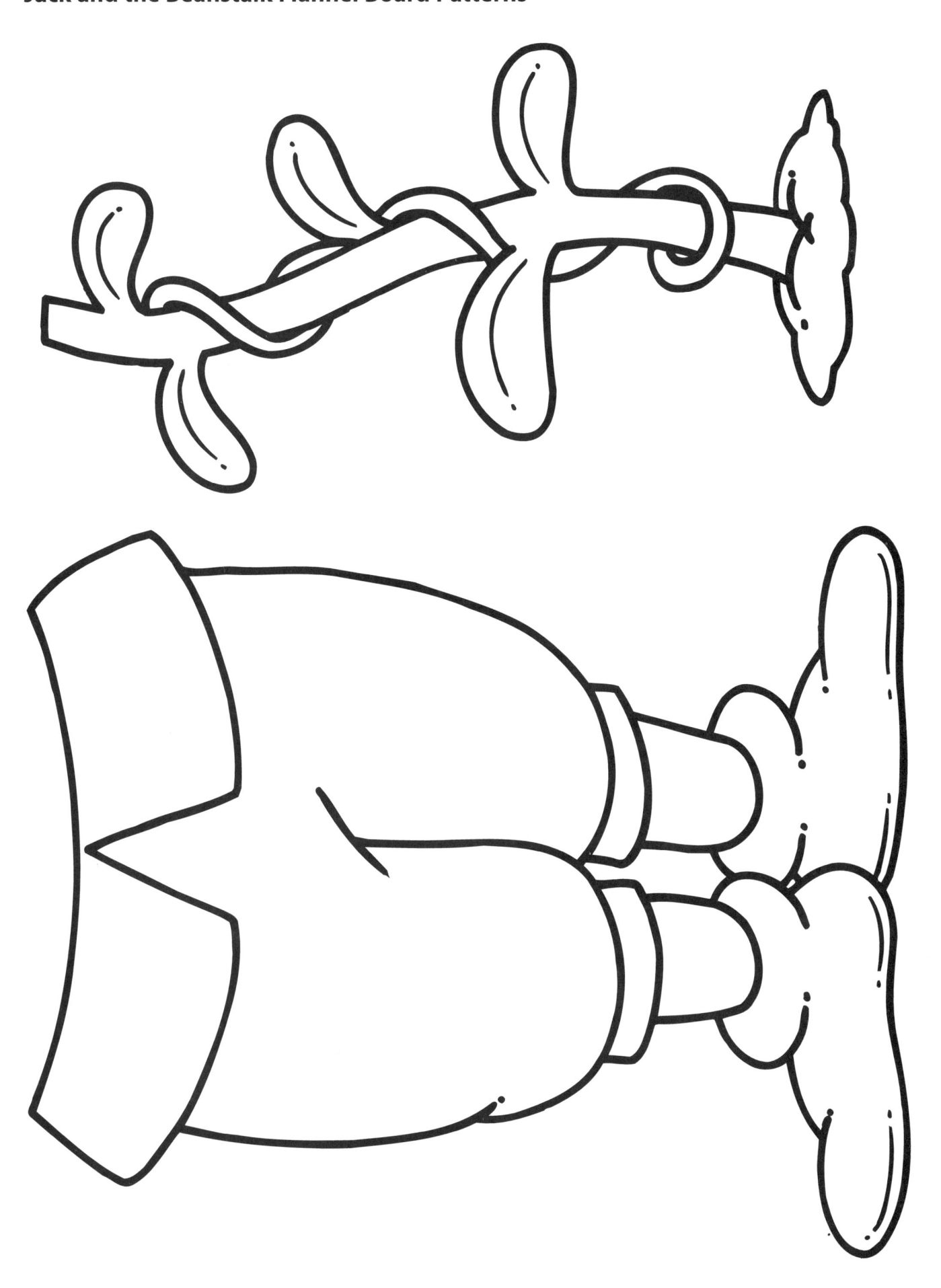

Newbridge 37

Life Science/Following Directions

PLANTING A BEANSTALK

You need:
- dry lima beans
- 6-oz. clear plastic cups
- paper towels
- sand
- water

1. Give each child several dry lima beans and a clear plastic cup.
2. Show children how to roll paper towels into cylinders and place them inside their plastic cups.
3. Help children pour about 1/4 cup of sand into the bottom of the cups, to secure the paper towels.
4. Have children drop in their beans between the paper towels and the sides of the cups.
5. Have children pour about 1/4 cup of water into their cups, wetting the sand at the bottom.
6. Set the plants in a window that receives some light. Have children water their bean seeds daily and watch for them to sprout. As the plants begin to sprout, children will be able to see the roots grow down toward the bottom of the cup and tiny leaves grow up toward the top. Be sure to grow some communal plants as well, as substitutes for any student's plant that may not grow.

Word Meanings/Vocabulary/Comparing and Contrasting

A STORY OF OPPOSITES

"Jack and the Beanstalk" is a story full of opposites. Give children the following examples of opposites from the story and ask them to name other instances of these opposites. Then have children look around the classroom to find other examples of opposites. If desired, let children illustrate some of the opposites from the story.

SAD and **HAPPY**— Jack was sad to have to sell the cow; he was happy to find the hen that had belonged to his father.

OLD and YOUNG— The little man was old; Jack was young.

EMPTY and **FULL**— Jack's stomach was empty at the beginning of the story; at the end it was full.

SHORT and **TALL**— Jack was short; the giant was tall.

LITTLE and **BIG**— Jack's house was little; the giant's house was big.

POOR and **RICH**— Jack was poor at the beginning of the story; he was rich at the end of the story.

Math/Counting/Sorting/Addition and Subtraction to 20/Art

BUNCHES OF BEANS ART PROJECT

You need:
- dried beans of different types: kidney, lima, pinto
- dishpan
- small cups, pitchers, and spoons
- construction paper
- glue

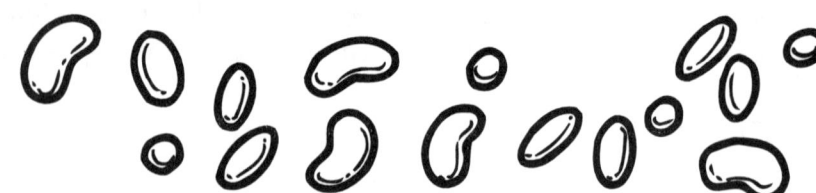

1. Pour all the dried beans into a dishpan.
2. Let children separate the beans using small cups, pitchers, and spoons.
3. Use the beans to practice beginning math skills with the class. Children may count out various amounts of beans up to 20, use the beans to illustrate simple math equations, or other activities.
4. Give children an assortment of beans, construction paper, and glue and tell the class to create a picture or design by gluing beans to paper.

Life Science/Art/Critical Thinking/Comparing/Observing

SPRING PLANTING CENTER

You need:
- butcher paper
- plastic cups
- watering can
- potting soil
- magnifying glass
- various plants and seeds
- crayons or markers
- scissors
- green construction paper
- tape

1. Label a wall or a bulletin board in the classroom "Spring Planting Center."
2. Cover a large table in the center with butcher paper and assemble the following supplies: plastic cups, watering can, potting soil, magnifying glass, various plants (flowering plant, ivy, etc.), and assorted seeds.
3. Let each child choose one flower pattern from pages 42 and 43. Reproduce the selected pattern once for each child. Have children color and cut out.
4. Give children green construction paper to use to make stems and leaves for the flowers. Have children tape the flowers in place.
5. Ask children what they think plants need in order to grow. (Be sure that children have included water, light, air, and soil/sand.) Record their answers and then write them on the flowers.
6. Hang the flowers on the wall or bulletin board in the Spring Planting Center.
7. Let children explore the Spring Planting Center in their free time. Encourage them to examine and compare the different seeds and plants.
8. For activities, see Planting Experiments on page 44 and Spring Planting Terrarium on page 45.

Flower Pattern

Newbridge 42

Flower Pattern

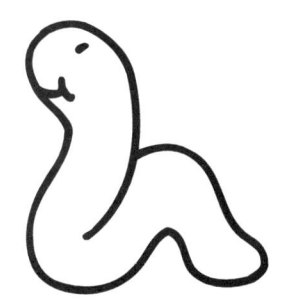

Newbridge 43

Life Science/Experimenting/Forming Hypotheses/Drawing Conclusions

PLANTING EXPERIMENTS

1. Cut the tops off three cardboard milk or juice containers and fill with soil.
2. Make a few holes in the soil and drop some seeds into each hole. Water.
3. Label the containers "Plant 1," "Plant 2," and "Plant 3."
4. Ask children to predict what will happen if the plants are given (a) too much water and light, (b) too little water and light, and (c) just the right amount of water and light. Write down the responses on chart paper. Tell children their guesses are called hypotheses.
5. Explain to children that they will be doing an experiment to find out if they predicted the right answers. Tell them this process is called testing their hypotheses.
6. Have children place Plant 1 in a dark closet. This plant will not be given water. Have children place Plant 2 under a continuous light source and water it every morning and afternoon. Have children place Plant 3 on a sunny windowsill and water every other day or as needed.
7. Let children observe the plants every day. Write the results on chart paper and post on a wall or a bulletin board.
8. After two weeks, take all three plants out and line them up. Ask children to describe the appearance of each plant. Check back to their original hypotheses and compare them with the results.

Life Science/Small Motor Skills

SPRING PLANTING TERRARIUM

You need:
- crayons or markers
- scissors
- glue
- 2- and 3-liter plastic bottles with removable bottoms
- soil
- sand
- small stones or pebbles
- seeds
- tape

1. Have children choose one of the terrarium covers on page 46. Reproduce the selected cover twice for each child. Have children color and cut out.
2. Show children how to glue the two strips of the covers end to end so one long strip is formed.
3. Give each child a 2- or 3-liter plastic bottle. Have children wash the bottles and peel off the labels.
4. Tell children to pull off the removable bottoms of the bottles. Then have each child cut off the top and bottom of each bottle, as shown.
5. Let children work at the Spring Planting Center. Show children how to fill the removable bottoms of the bottles with soil and sand. Then have children place some stones or pebbles into the mixtures.
6. Show children how to create shallow holes by pressing their fingertips into the soil. Give each child one or two seeds to drop into each hole.
7. Have children water the soil and insert the bottles into the removable bottoms, as shown.
8. Invite each child to tape his or her terrarium cover strip in place around the bottom of the terrarium.

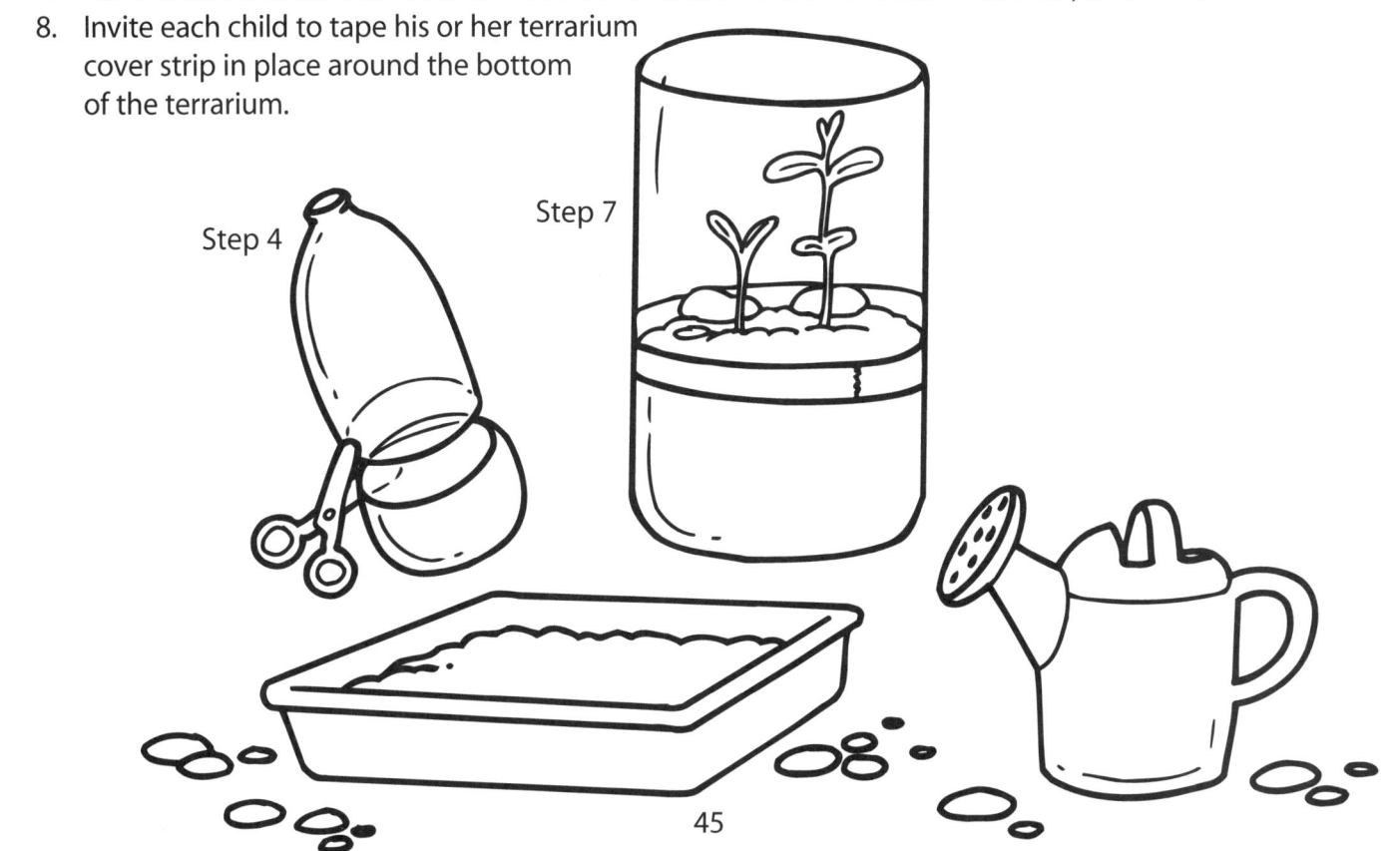

Terrarium Cover Patterns

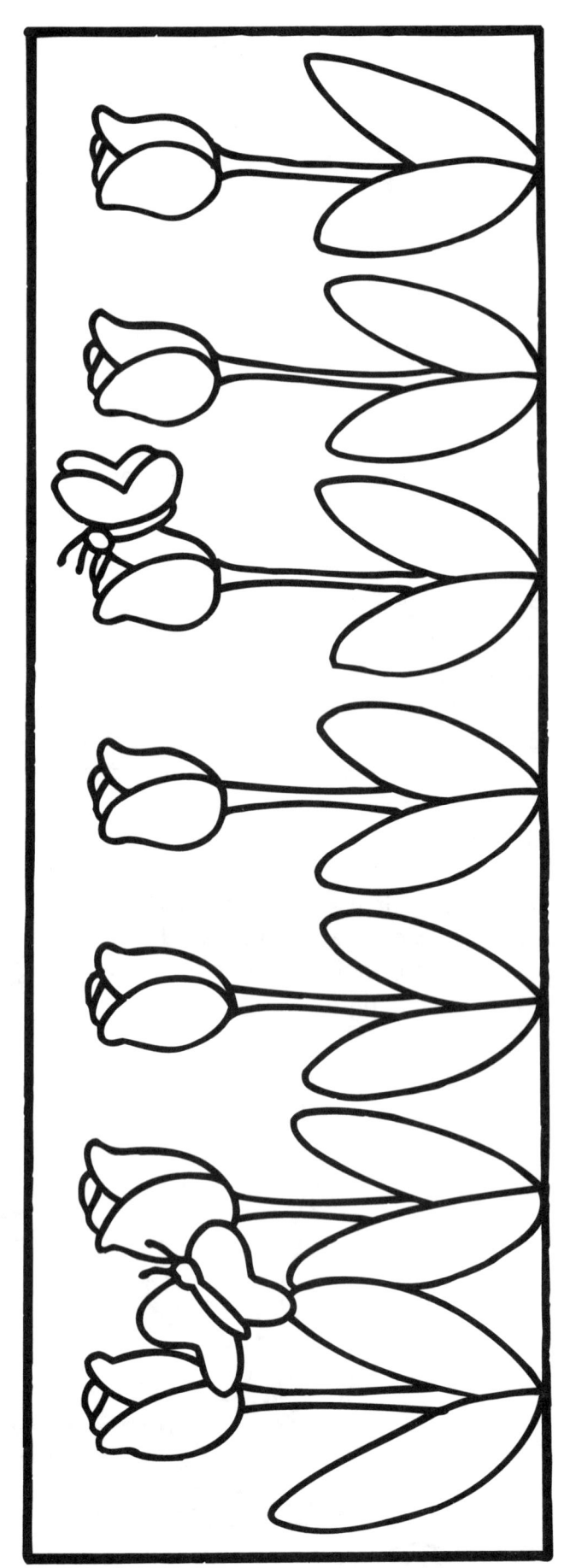

Newbridge　　　　　　　　　　46

Small Motor Skills/Large Motor Skills/Dramatic Play/Life Science

GROWING A GARDEN SONG AND GAME
(sung to the tune of "Here We Go 'Round the Mulberry Bush")

1. Reproduce either the marigold or the sunflower pattern on pages 42 and 43 for each child. Have children color, cut out, and decorate.
2. Punch a hole in the petal of each child's flower and thread a 20" length of yarn through it. Knot the ends. While children are wearing their pendants, teach them the following song and accompanying movements.

This is the way we dig the soil, (*children pretend to dig*)
Dig the soil, dig the soil.
This is the way we dig the soil,
So we can make a garden.

This is the way we plant the seeds… (*children pretend to drop seeds down*)

This is the way we water the soil… (*children pretend to sprinkle water*)

This is the way we give it sun… (*children pretend to be the sun*)

This is the way we watch it grow… (*children hold up flowers*)

This is the way we pull the weeds… (*children pretend to pull weeds*)

Art/Small Motor Skills/Life Science/Classifying/Sorting

SPRING GARDEN BULLETIN BOARD

You need:
- bulletin board paper
- crayons or markers
- scissors
- stapler

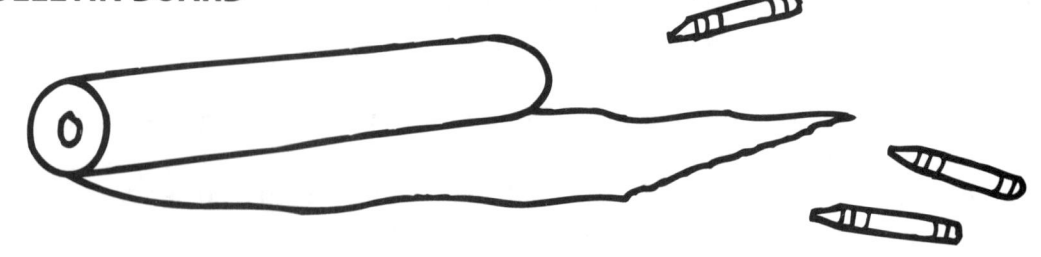

1. Reproduce each pattern on pages 49 through 51 several times, depending on how many vegetables you want to appear in your bulletin board garden. Make sure you reproduce at least one pattern for each child. Have children color and cut out the patterns.
2. Talk about the ways that vegetables grow. Explain that a vegetable's roots grow under the ground while its stems and leaves grow above the ground. The part of the vegetable that we eat is either above or below the ground in the garden, depending on whether we eat the roots, stems, or leaves.
3. Draw a long horizontal line on the bulletin board paper to represent the ground. Then help children place the vegetables properly on the bulletin board. Carrots, beets, radishes, potatoes, and onions should appear beneath the line; corn, lettuce, tomatoes, and green beans should appear above the line. Staple all patterns to the bulletin board.

Vegetable Patterns

Vegetable Patterns

Newbridge 50

Vegetable Patterns

Newbridge 51

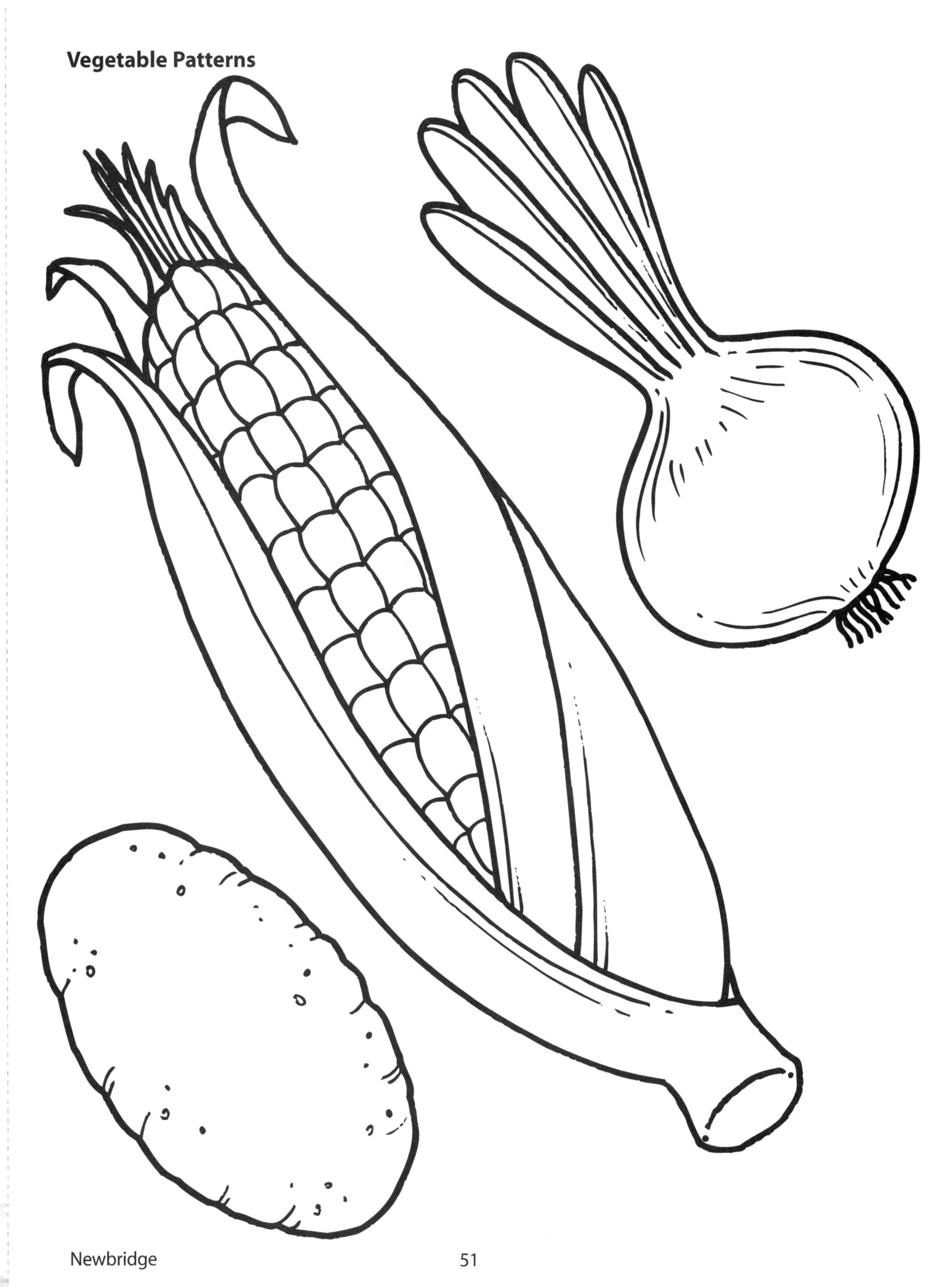

GROW-A-PLANT BOOK

Name _____

Color the pictures and cut them out. Put the pictures in the right order. Then staple them together to make a book.

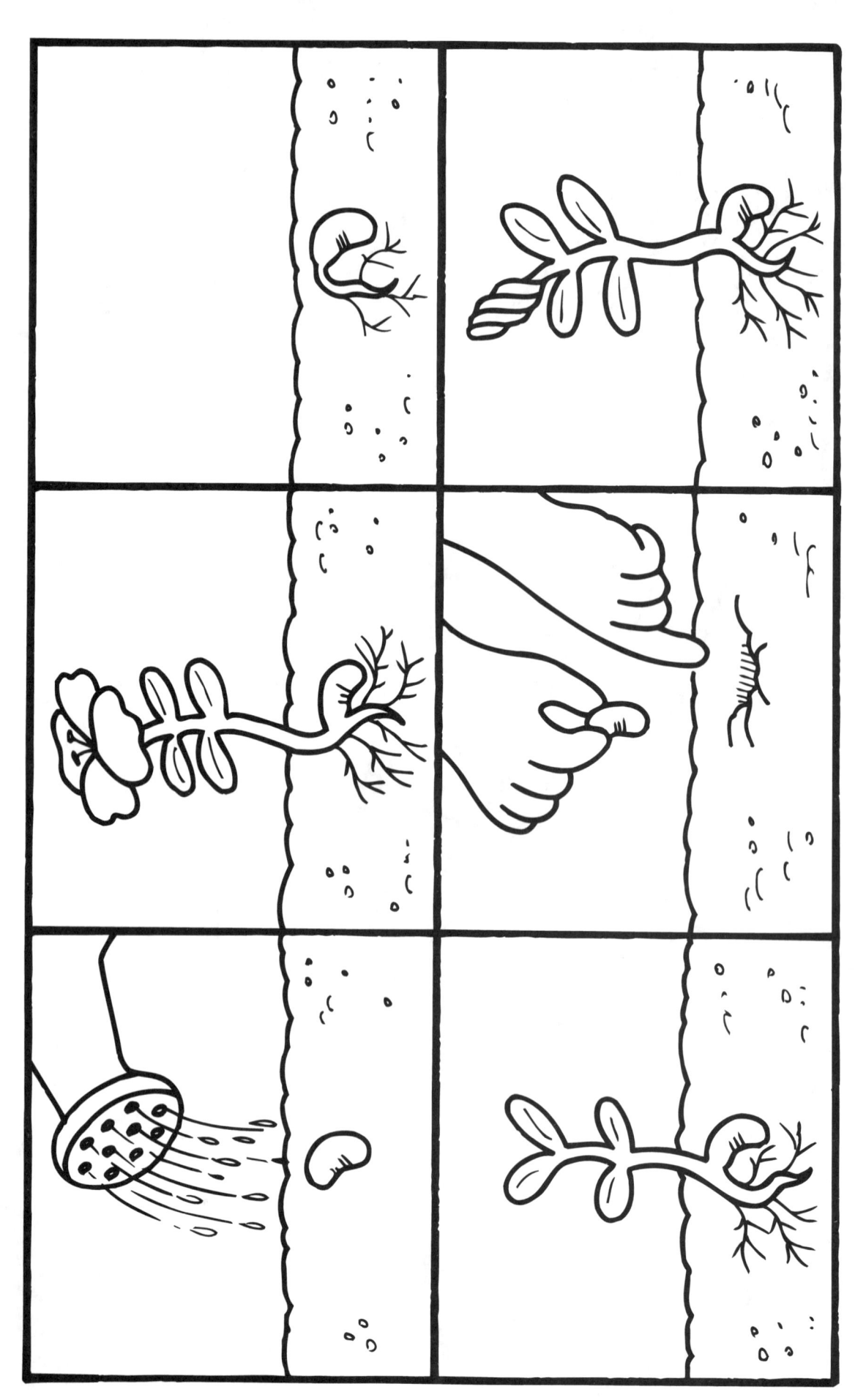

Literature Connection/Reading

RECOMMENDED READING

Read some of the following books about gardens to your class. Keep the books on a reading table or in a bookcase so that children may look at them during free time.

The Carrot Seed by Ruth Kraus, published by HarperCollins.
The Giant Vegetable Garden by Nadine Bernard Westcott, published by Little, Brown.
How My Garden Grew by Anne Rockwell, published by Macmillan.
Mr. Mead and His Garden by John Vernon Lord, published by Houghton Mifflin.
Rabbit Seeds by Bijou Le Tord, published by Macmillan.
This Year's Garden by Cynthia Rylant, published by Macmillan.

Science/Art/Small Motor Skills

SPRING SCIENCE CENTERS

You need:
- crayons or markers
- glue
- oaktag
- scissors
- tape or stapler

1. Reproduce all the science-center patterns on pages 56, 58, and 60 once. Color, mount on oaktag, and cut out.
2. Attach each science-center sign to a wall, bulletin board, or work center in a different area of the classroom.
3. For the Life Science Center, cut out pictures from magazines that include plants, animals, and people. Create a collage around the center and ask children to contribute pictures of their own. See page 55 for an activity to set up in the center.
4. For the Earth Science Center, collect pictures of different environments such as desert, forest, polar region, etc. You may also add weather pictures, volcanoes, and outer-space pictures. Again, encourage children to cut out and add pictures of their own. See 57 for an activity to set up in the center.
5. For the Physical Science Center, cut out pictures of bubbles, magnets, hot-air balloons, simple machines, etc. See page 59 for an activity to set up in the center.

Life Science/Recording Information

LIFE SCIENCE—GROWING UP AND DOWN

You need:
- potting soil
- seeds
- magnifying glass
- clear plastic cups

1. Give each child a clear plastic cup and show them how to fill it 3/4 of the way with potting soil.
2. Distribute seeds to each child in the class. Show children how to plant the seeds about 1/2" deep and at the edge of the cup so they are still visible.
3. Ask the children what plants need in order to grow, and make a list on chart paper ("air, sunlight, water").
4. Place the cups near the window and allow children time each week to water their seeds. In a few days they will be able to see the roots of the plant.
5. Tilt the cups by placing small rocks under one side of the cup. This will encourage the roots to grow toward the side of the cup, so children can see them more clearly. Invite children to examine the roots with the magnifying glass.
6. Have children keep picture journals of their root and seedling growth.

Science Center Pattern

LIFE SCIENCE

Newbridge

56

Earth Science/Color Recognition

EARTH SCIENCE—MAKING RAINBOWS

Ask children if they know where rainbows come from. Explain that rainbows happen when light from the sun passes through raindrops or drops of moisture. That is why we usually see rainbows after it rains. Sunlight may look like just one color, but it is actually made up of many colors: red, orange, yellow, green, blue, indigo, and violet. When the light passes through the raindrop, it splits into all those colors. Tell children that you can make your own classroom rainbow.

You need:
- clear glass jar
- water
- white paper

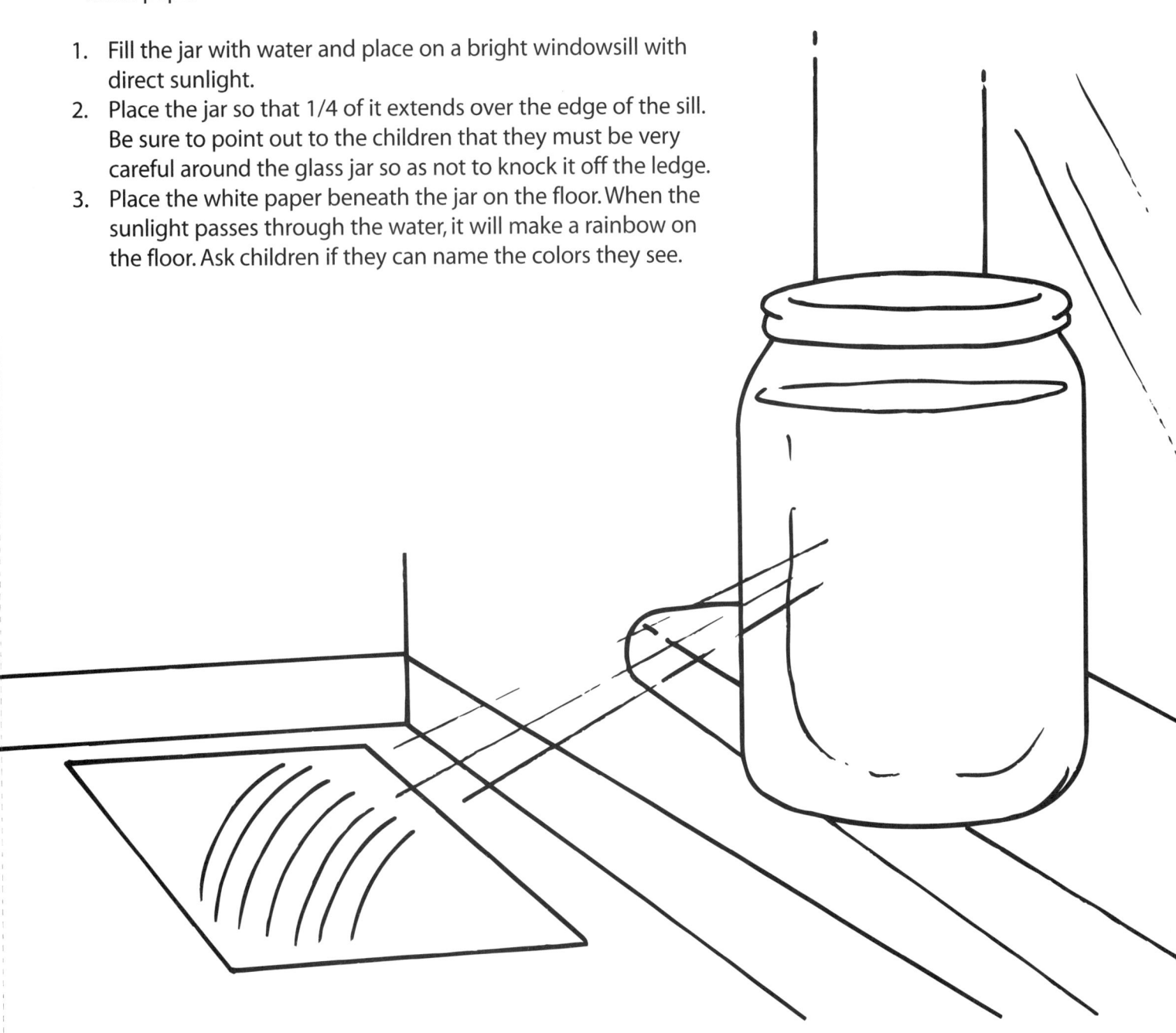

1. Fill the jar with water and place on a bright windowsill with direct sunlight.
2. Place the jar so that 1/4 of it extends over the edge of the sill. Be sure to point out to the children that they must be very careful around the glass jar so as not to knock it off the ledge.
3. Place the white paper beneath the jar on the floor. When the sunlight passes through the water, it will make a rainbow on the floor. Ask children if they can name the colors they see.

Science Center Pattern

EARTH SCIENCE

Newbridge

Physical Science/Learning About Magnets/Predicting/Drawing Conclusions

PHYSICAL SCIENCE—ATTRACTING OTHERS!

Ask children what they know about magnets. Show children that each magnet has two ends—a north pole and a south pole. North poles are always attracted to south poles, but the two north poles (and two south poles) of the magnet repel, or move away from, each other. Gather an assortment of different objects, both metal and nonmetal, and place two magnets in the center.

Ask children to predict which objects the magnets will pick up. Record their answers on chart paper and then allow the children time to experiment. Which objects did the magnets pick up? Which ones did they not pick up? What do all the objects that were attracted to the magnets have in common? What were they made out of?

Science Center Pattern

Newbridge

Art/Small Motor Skills

BIRTHDAY PARTY PARADE HATS

You need:
- glue
- oaktag
- scissors
- crayons or markers
- decorating materials (glitter, stickers, tissue paper)
- 2" x 24" strips of construction paper
- stapler

1. When a student has a birthday, let him or her choose one of the birthday hat patterns on pages 63 through 65. Reproduce the selected pattern, mount on oaktag, and cut out.
2. Let the birthday child color and decorate his or her hat using crayons or markers and other materials such as glitter, stickers, and tissue paper.
3. Give the child a 2" x 24" strip of construction paper. Have the child fold the strip in half and glue the hat to the center, as shown. Staple to fit around the birthday child's head.
4. Before the end of the school day, have all the children in the class and the birthday child's teachers sign their names on the inside of the hat. Write the date on the hat and give it to the child to take home.
5. For other activities, see Birthday Party Parade on page 62.

Large Motor Skills/Dramatic Play

BIRTHDAY PARTY PARADE

Have the birthday child wear his or her birthday hat and lead a parade around the classroom while the rest of the class sings the chant below. Encourage the birthday child to make various movements to go along with the words in the chant.

Hip, hip, hurray! Hip, hip, hurray!
(*Name*) is (*number*) years old today!
Hip, hip, hurray! Hip, hip, hurray!
(*Name*) is (*number*) years old today!
First (*name*) goes fast.
Then (*name*) goes slow.
(*Name*) touches high.
Then (*name*) touches low.
(*Name*) can turn round and round.
Clap (*his/her*) hands, and then sit down!

Birthday Hat Pattern

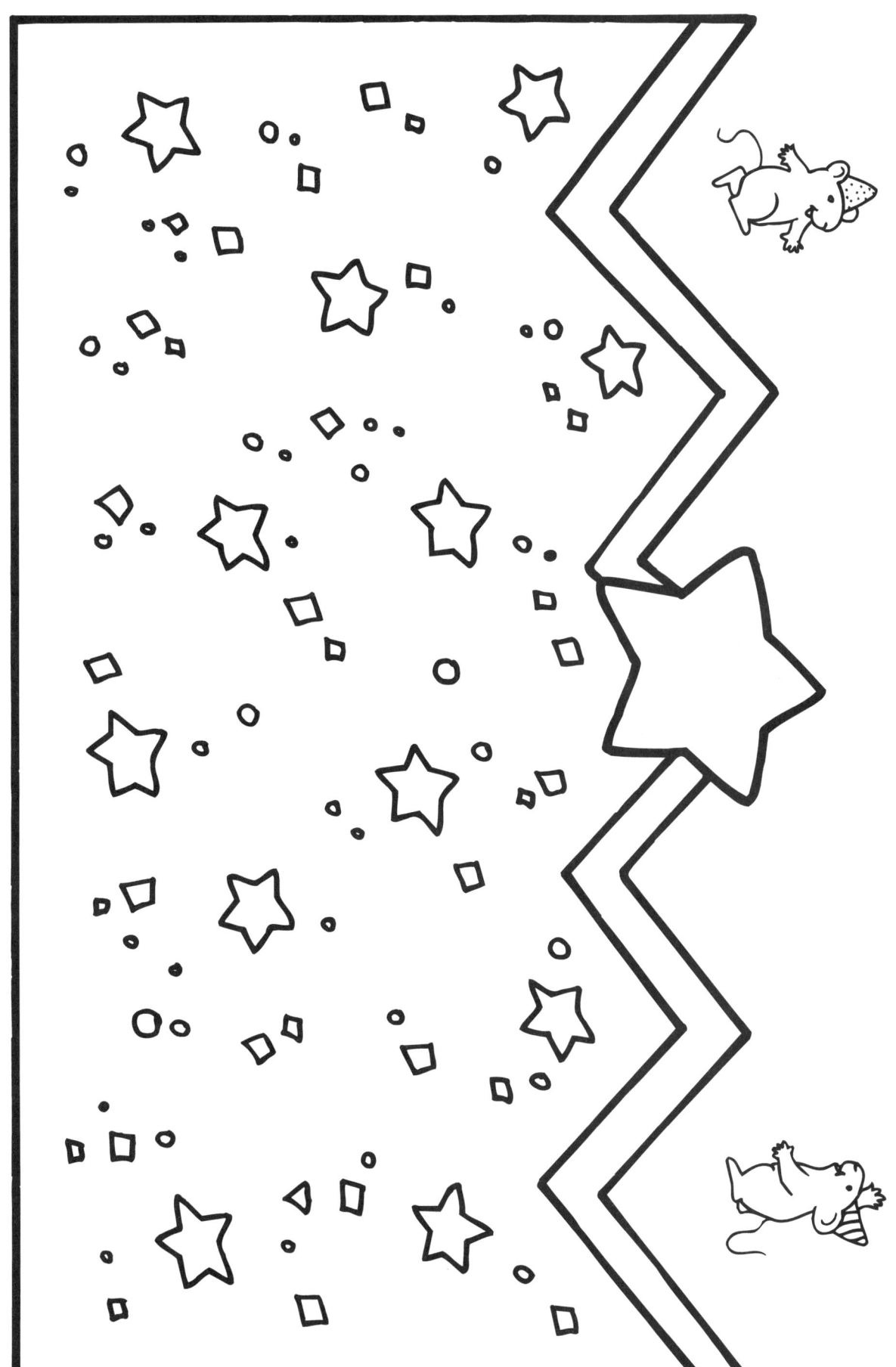

Newbridge 63

Birthday Hat Pattern

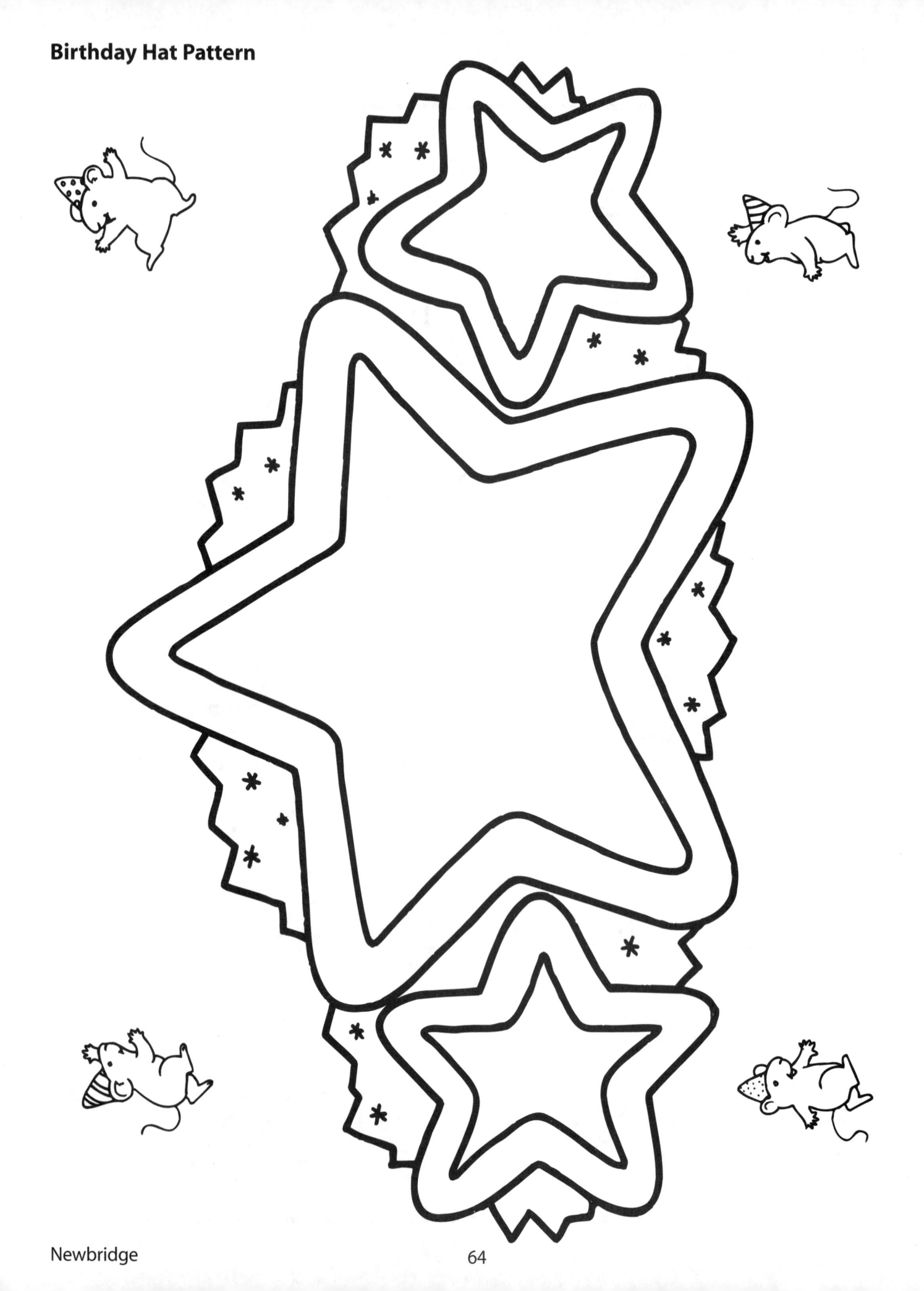

Newbridge

64

Birthday Hat Pattern

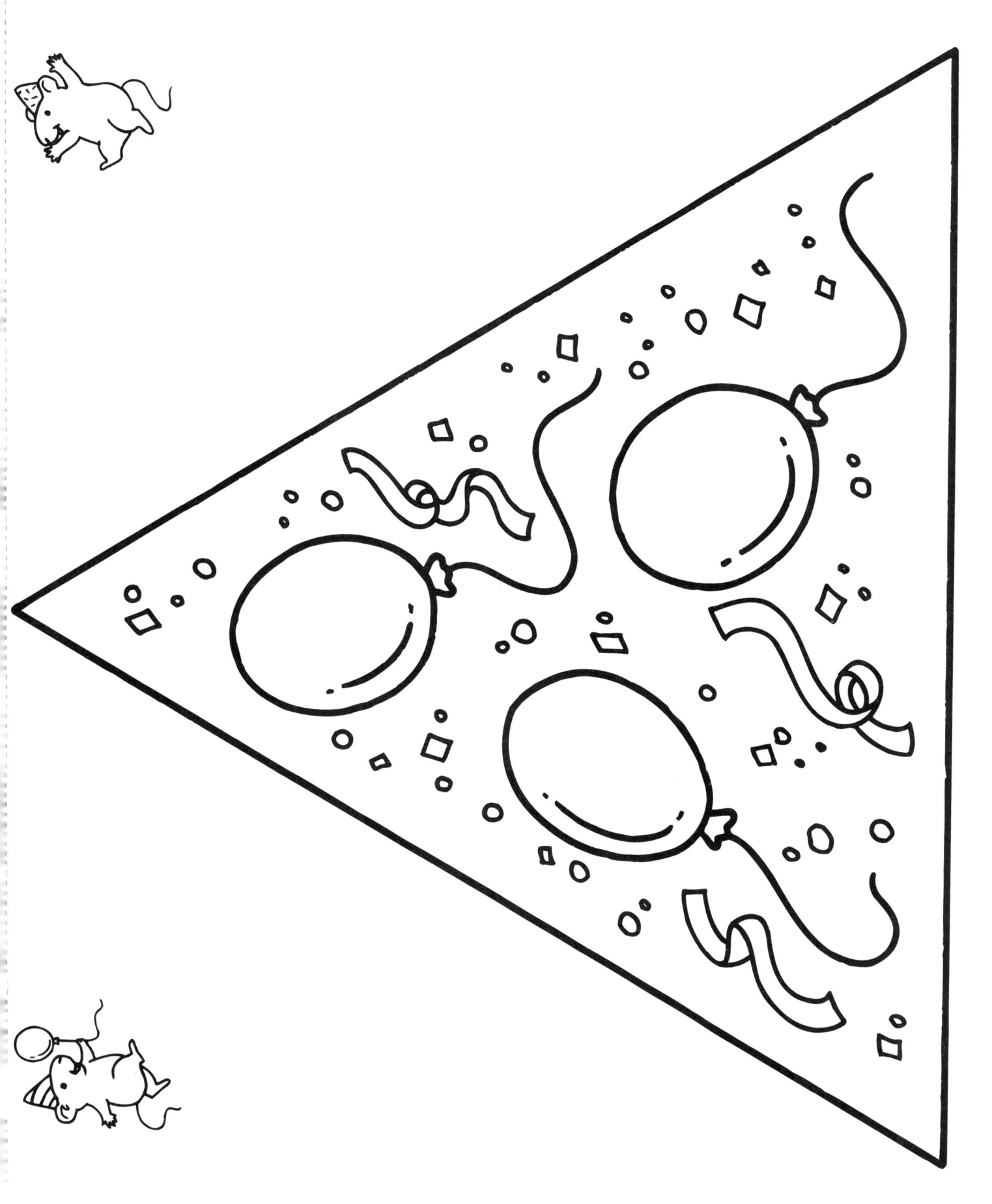

Newbridge 65

Art/Small Motor Skills/Social Skills

AN UNBIRTHDAY PARTY

Invite all the children in the class whose birthdays do not fall during periods of school to choose a hat pattern and decorate it. Explain that the class will be celebrating their "unbirthdays," since their birthdays do not fall during school periods.

1. If parents usually supply treats on birthdays, ask the parents of the "unbirthday" children to contribute something for the party, such as cups, drinks, napkins, party favors, snacks, and so on.
2. Serve the Birthday Ice-Cream Cookie on page 67 to the class.
3. Create the Birthday Party Parade Hats per the instructions on page 61.
4. Let all the children participate in the Birthday Party Parade (see page 62).

Cooking/Following Directions

BIRTHDAY ICE-CREAM COOKIE

You need:
- 9" x 13" pan
- two rolls of slice-and-bake cookie dough
- gallon of ice cream

Optional:
decorative cake icing

1. Unwrap the cookie dough and have children pat it down in the bottom of a 9" x 13" pan.
2. Bake the dough for 25 to 30 minutes at 350° F.
3. Let the dough cool for approximately 30 minutes to an hour. Meanwhile, soften the ice cream for 30 minutes to an hour.
4. Let children take turns spreading the softened ice cream over the baked dough. If desired, use decorative cake icing to write a birthday message.
5. Freeze the mixture until hard (1 to 2 hours).
6. Remove from freezer 5 to 10 minutes before serving, then cut into squares and serve. Serves 15 to 20 children.

Small Motor Skills/Following Directions

SUPERMARKET FILE-FOLDER GAME

HOW TO MAKE

You need:
- crayons or markers
- scissors
- glue
- letter-sized file folder
- envelope
- oaktag
- clear contact paper
- die

1. Reproduce the game board pattern on pages 70 and 71 once. Reproduce the game cards and shopping cart marker on page 72 four times. Color and cut out.
2. Glue the game board to the inside of a letter-sized file folder. Glue an envelope to the back of the folder.
3. Mount the game cards and playing pieces on oaktag. Color, laminate, and cut out.
4. Store the game cards and playing pieces in the envelope on the back of the folder.

Nutrition/Counting/Classifying/Sorting/Following Directions

SUPERMARKET FILE-FOLDER GAME

HOW TO PLAY
(for 2 to 4 players)

1. The youngest player goes first. He or she rolls the die and moves the shopping cart marker the number of spaces indicated.
2. If the player lands on a space featuring a picture of food from one of the four food groups, the player gets that food group card. If the player lands on a space featuring a picture of a junk food, the player loses a turn.
3. Play continues clockwise around the board. When one player has collected cards for all four food groups, he or she must then move forward on the game board to one of the paths leading to the checkout counter.
4. The first player to collect all four food group cards and reach the checkout is the winner.

yogurt

CHECKO

SODA

Newbridge 70

wheat Flakes
POTATO CHIPS
BUTTER
POPCORN
OUT
CANDY
OATMEAL
START

Supermarket File-Folder Game Cards and Marker Patterns

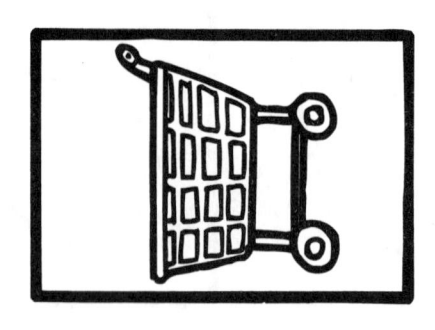

Newbridge

72

Nutrition/Art/Small Motor Skills

WHAT PEOPLE EAT CLASS BOOK

1. Talk about favorite foods. Ask each child to write or dictate a list of his or her family's favorite foods. Each child might also ask friends outside the class which foods they like best. If possible, take a neighborhood walk to see the types of foods sold in stores. Write down all the information on chart paper.
2. Display books about food from all over the world for group and individual reading.
3. Give each child a plain white paper plate. Have each child pick a food about which he or she would like to draw and write on the plate. If desired, let children cut out pictures from magazines featuring their chosen food.
4. If any food group has been missed, ask volunteers to make up these plates.
5. Tie or staple the plates together at one edge. Choose several children to design a cover for the book. Show the completed book to the class and discuss how many different foods there are in the world.

Art/Small Motor Skills/Nutrition

FLOWER FRUIT SALAD

1. Ask each child to bring in one piece of fruit from home.
2. Divide the class into four food preparation groups: Washers, Cutters, Peelers, and Servers. The Washers will rinse off the fruit as required; the Cutters will cut up fruit into chunks or slices; the Peelers will peel fruit with skins; and the Servers will prepare plates for each table with equal amounts of fruit on them.
3. Help the class arrange their fruit to look like flowers using the following suggestions: banana slices forming a circle in the middle, apple slices radiating out from them, and a grape at the outside tip of each apple slice; a grape in the middle with orange slices radiating out from it.
4. Encourage children to make their own fruit flowers and show to the other members of the class.

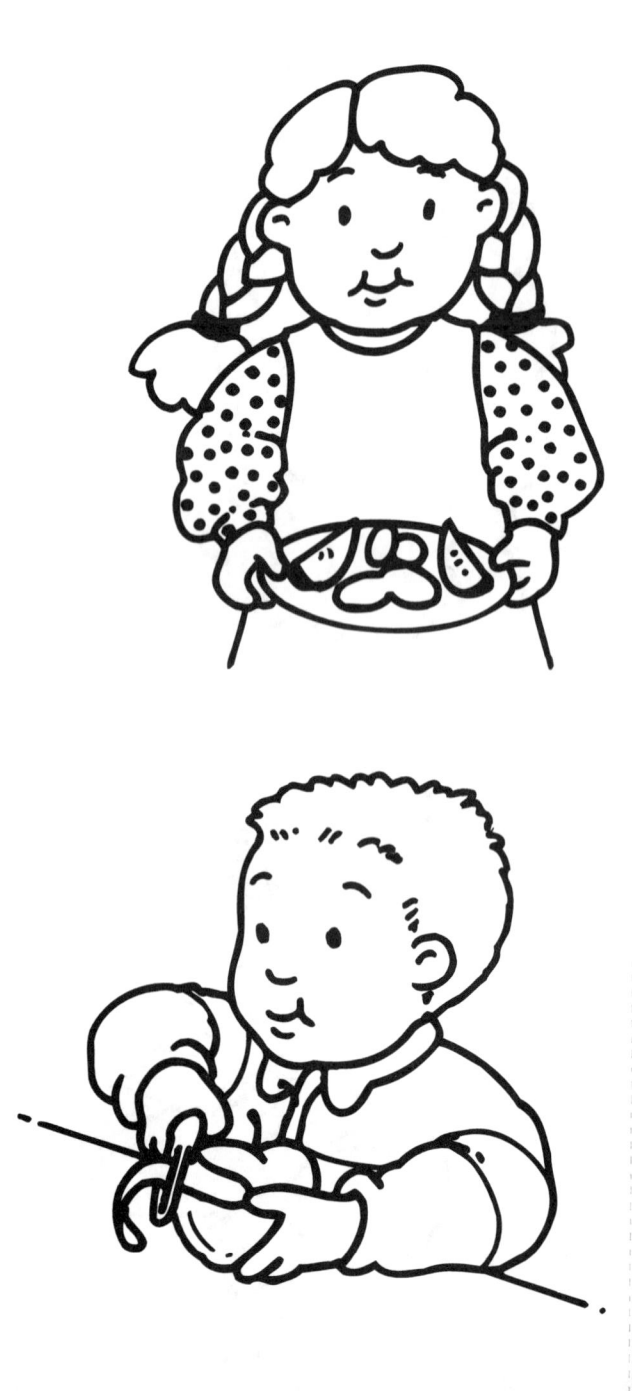

Large Motor Skills/Nutrition/Sorting

FOOD GROUP BENDER GAME

(for 3 to 6 players)

1. Reproduce the game cards on page 72 ten times. Have children color and cut out.
2. Cut forty oaktag circles 7" in diameter. Glue one game card to the middle of each circle.
3. Arrange the circles in rows on the floor, placing cards of the same food group in each row about 8" apart. Lay the rows about 8" apart and tape the circles securely to the floor.
4. To make the spinner, divide an 8" x 8" piece of oaktag into four quadrants. Cut out pictures from magazines of foods from each of the four food groups. Glue one food-group picture in each quadrant. Punch a hole in the middle and attach an oaktag arrow with a brass fastener.
5. Players stand on the edge of the playing area. The leader spins the arrow and calls out the food group it lands on. Each player must place a foot or a hand on a circle with that food group on it. The players then use whatever free hand or foot they have for consecutive spins. If a player has no free hand or foot, he or she is permitted to move a hand or a foot already placed on a circle.
6. If a player falls, he or she is out. The last upright player is the winner.

75

Art/Small Motor Skills

HIDE-AND-SEEK SNAIL

You need:
- crayons or markers
- scissors
- oaktag
- glue
- stapler
- craft sticks
- plastic straws

1. Have children choose one of the snail head and body patterns from page 77 or 78. Reproduce once for each child. Have children color and cut out.
2. Reproduce the shell pattern on page 79 once for each child. Have children color and cut out.
3. Show the class how to trace the snail head, body, and shell onto oaktag and cut out. Have children glue the snail head onto the body, as shown.
4. Have each child glue a craft stick to the back of the shell, as shown.
5. Help each child staple a straw to the end of the snail body, as shown.
6. Place the shell on top of a piece of oaktag and glue around the edges, leaving 7" openings on opposite sides of the shell.
7. Show children how to insert the snail head and body through the openings in the back of the shell. Demonstrate how to manipulate the snail in and out of its shell by pushing and pulling on the straw.
8. For activities, see Who's Hiding? on page 80.

Snail Head and Body Patterns

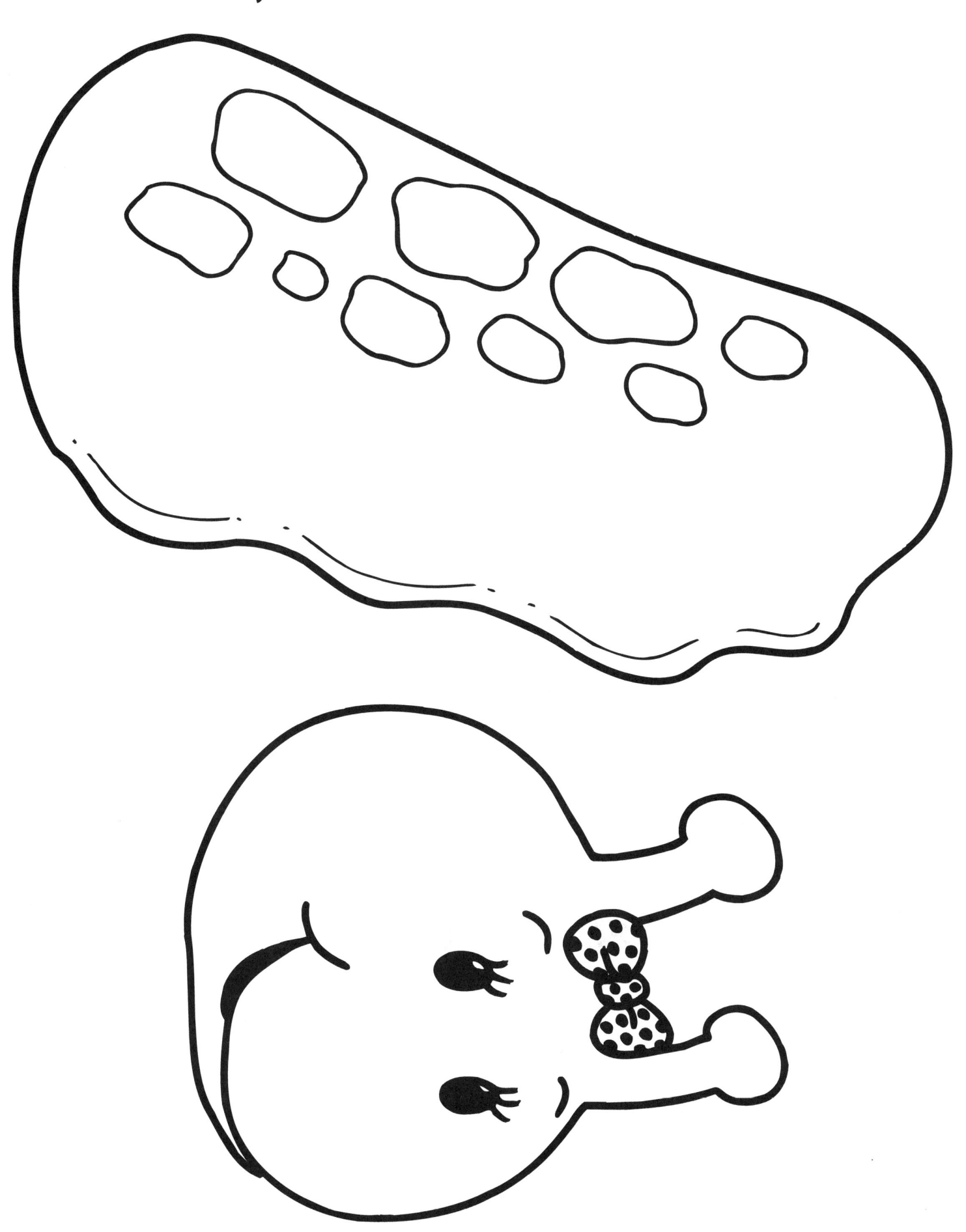

Newbridge 77

Snail Head and Body Patterns

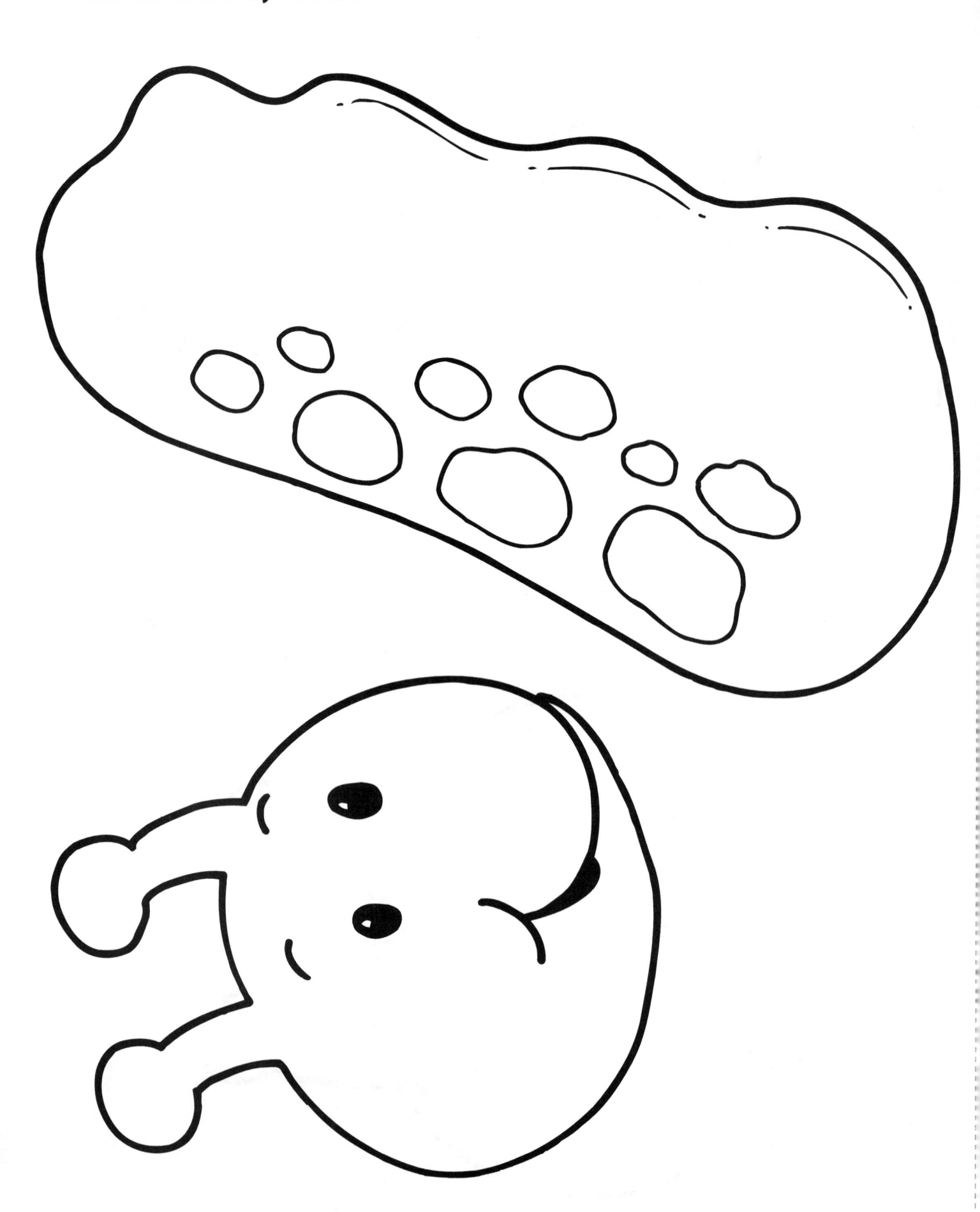

Newbridge 78

Snail Shell Pattern

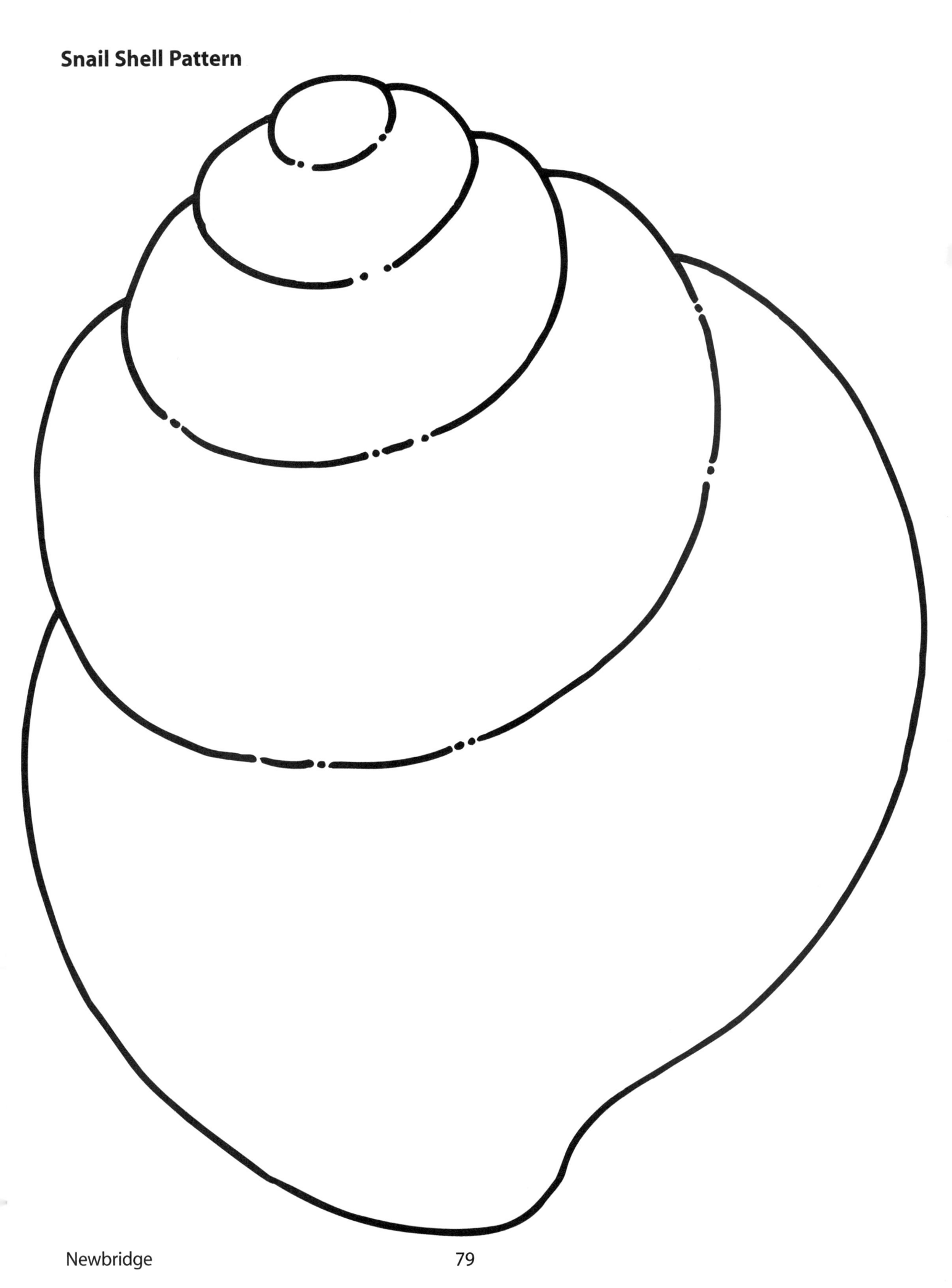

Newbridge 79

Science/Critical Thinking/Visual Discrimination

SNAIL TALK

Share these interesting facts about snails with your class.

1. Find out from children what they know about snails. Ask the class if they know how a snail moves around. Explain how its "foot," the body of the snail, excretes a slime that allows the foot to glide over surfaces.
2. Tell children that the snail's body is very tough. It can climb over the sharp edge of a razor and not cut itself. Also, a snail never gets lost. It knows from the time it is born how to find its way. This is called instinct.
3. Snails weigh less than half an ounce, but they can pull something weighing more than one pound. Have children hold an object comparable to a snail's weight, like a penny or a small ball of dough. In their other hand, have them hold an object weighing a pound, like a large building block.
4. The snail's tongue has hundreds of tiny teeth on it for cutting and shredding the plants it eats.
5. The snail has two large feelers called tentacles with eyes at the very top. There are also two smaller feelers closer to the mouth used mostly for smelling.
6. A snail's shell is used as its home. When the weather is too dry outside, the snail seals up the open side of its shell and stays inside until the area becomes wetter. A snail also uses its shell as protection. If something happens to frighten the snail, it will go inside its shell, where it is safe.

WHO'S HIDING?

Ask children if they know of other animals besides snails who can hide inside their shells. Explain that a snail or other hiding animal will go inside its shell when it becomes frightened or feels danger. That way, nothing can get inside the shell to hurt the snail. Then play the following game with the class.

1. Have the class sit holding up their snail puppets (see page 76). Choose one child to be "it." The rest of the snails will hide inside their shells while "it" turns around.
2. When "it" has his or her back turned, point to one child. He or she will poke the snail back out of its shell.
3. Then the class says, "Come out, snail!" At that moment "it" will turn around and have till the count of three to name the child holding the snail who is not hiding. (If the count of three is too short or long for the class, change it accordingly.)
4. The child chosen will then take a turn regardless of whether or not "it" named him or her.